Imaginative writing

impact

WRITING HOMEWORK

Published by Scholastic Ltd,
Villiers House,
Clarendon Avenue,
Leamington Spa,
Warwickshire CV32 5PR

© 1996 Scholastic Ltd
1 2 3 4 5 6 7 8 9 0 6 7 8 9 0 1 2 3 4 5
Text © 1996 University of
North London Enterprises Ltd

UNIVERSITY OF
NORTH LONDON

Activities by the IMPACT Project at the
University of North London, collated and
rewritten by Ruth Merttens, Alan Newland
and Susie Webb

Editor Jane Bishop
Assistant editor Ben Orme
Designer Claire Belcher
Series designer Anna Oliwa
Illustrations James Alexander
Cover illustration Headlines, Charlbury, Oxford

Designed using Aldus Pagemaker
Printed in Great Britain by Clays Ltd, Bungay, Suffolk

British Library Cataloguing-in-Publication Data
A catalogue record for this book is available from the British Library.

ISBN 0-590 53371-1

Extract from WE'RE GOING ON A BEAR HUNT.
Text © 1989 Michael Rosen. Illustrations ©1989 Helen Oxenbury.
Permission granted by the publisher Walker Books Limited.

impact
WRITING HOMEWORK

KEY STAGE ONE

CONTENTS

impact

WRITING HOMEWORK

impact
INTRODUCTION

IMPACT books are designed to help teachers involve parents in children's learning to write. Through the use of interesting and specially developed writing tasks, parents can encourage and support their child's efforts as they become confident and competent writers.

The shared writing programme is modelled on the same process as the IMPACT shared maths which encompasses a non-traditional approach to homework.

This is outlined in the following diagram:

> The teacher selects a task based on the work she is doing in class. The activity may relate to the children's work in a particular topic, to the type of writing they are engaged in or to their reading.

> The teacher prepares the children for what they have to do at home. This may involve reading a particular story, playing a game or having a discussion with the children about the task.

> The children take home the activity, and share it with someone at home. This may be an older brother/sister, a parent or grandparent or any other friend or relation.

> The parents and children respond to the activity by commenting in an accompanying diary or notebook.
> * This mechanism provides the teacher with valuable feedback.

> The teacher uses what was done at home as the basis for follow-up work in class. This may involve further writing, drawing, reading or discussion.

The activities in this book have been designed to enable children to develop and expand their writing skills in conversation with those at home. Where possible the activities reflect the context of the home rather than the school, and draw upon experiences and events from out-of-school situations.

Shared activities – or homework with chatter!

Importantly, the activities are designed to be shared. Unlike traditional homework, where the child is expected to 'do it alone' and not to have help, with IMPACT they are encouraged – even required – to find someone to talk to and share the activity with. With each task we say the following should be true:

- something is said;
- something is written;
- something is read.

Sometimes the main point of the IMPACT activity is the discussion – and so we do try to encourage parents to see that the task involves a lot more than just completing a piece of writing. It is very important that teachers go through the task carefully with the children so that they know what to do. Clearly not all the children, or parents, will be able to read the instructions in English and so this preparation is crucial if the children are

to be able to share the activity. The sheet often acts more as a backup or a prompt than a recipe.

Diaries

The shared writing works by involving parents in their children's learning. The IMPACT diaries* are a crucial part of this process. They provide a mechanism by means of which an efficient parent-teacher-dialogue is established. These diaries enable teachers to obtain valuable feedback both about children's performances in relation to specific activities and about the tasks themselves. Parents are able to alert the teacher to any matter of concern or pleasant occurrences, and nothing is left to come as a big surprise or a horrible shock in the end of year report. It is difficult to exaggerate the importance of the IMPACT diaries. The OFSTED inspectors and HMI have highly commended their effectiveness in helping to raise children's achievements and in developing a real partnership with parents.
* See the Afterword (page 128) for details of where to obtain these.

Timing

Most schools send the Shared Writing activities fortnightly. Many interleave these activities with the IMPACT maths tasks, thus ensuring that the children have something to share with their parents almost every week. Many schools also use the shared writing tasks to enhance their shared reading or PACT programme. It has been found that some parents may be encouraged to take a renewed interest in reading a book with their child on a regular basis when the shared writing project is launched in a class. However, there are a variety of practices and the important point is that each teacher should feel comfortable with how often IMPACT is sent in her class.

Parent friendly

It is important for the success of the IMPACT Shared Writing that parents are aware of both the purpose and the extent of each activity. Many teachers adopt a developmental approach to writing, encouraging emergent writing or the use of invented spellings. Care has to be taken to share the philosophy behind this approach with parents, and to select activities which will not assume that parents are as familiar with the implications as teachers. You will get lots of support if parents can see that what they are doing is helping their child to become cheerful and successful writers!

To facilitate this process, each activity contains a note to parents which helps to make it clear what the purpose of the activity is, and how they can best help. The activities also contain hints to help parents share the activity in an enjoyable and effective manner. Sometimes the hints contain ideas, or starting points. On other occasions they may be examples or demonstrations of how to set about the task concerned.

It is always important to bear in mind that parents can, and sometimes should, do things differently at home. At home, many children will enjoy, and even benefit from, copying underneath a line of text or writing without paying attention to spelling or punctuation, where in school such things might not be expected or encouraged. The most successful partnerships between home and school recognise both the differences and the similarities in each other's endeavours.

Planning

The shared writing activities are divided into three sections according to age: Reception, Year 1 and Year 2. There are two pages of teachers' notes relating to the individual activities at the beginning of each section. When selecting which activity to send home with the children it is helpful to remember the following:

• Ideally, we send the same activity with each child in the class or year. The activities are mostly designed to be as open-ended as possible, to allow for a wide variety of different levels of response. Teachers often add a few extra comments of their own to a particular sheet to fit it to the needs of a particular child or group of children with special educational needs. It is also important to stress that the child does not have to do all the actual writing – often the parent does half or more. The point of the activity may lie in the discussion and the creation of a joint product.

• It is useful to send a variety of different activities. Some children will particularly enjoy a word game, while others will prefer a task which includes drawing a picture. Activities may be used to launch a topic, to support a particular project, to enable a good quality of follow-up to an idea and to revise or practise particular skills. Much of the benefit of the shared writing exercise may be derived from the follow-up work back in the classroom. Therefore, it is very important to select activities which will feed into the type of work being focused upon at that time. For example, if the class is working on grammatical categories, verbs, nouns, etc., then an activity requiring that children and parents produce real and fictional definitions of long words will fit in well. On the other hand, if the class is doing some work on fairy stories, making a **wanted** poster of a character in a story may be appropriate.

Notes to teachers

These give suggestions to the teachers. They outline what may be done before the activity is sent to ensure that it goes well at home. And they describe how the activity may be followed up as part of routine classwork during the subsequent week. More help with what happens when the activity comes back is to be found in the Afterword on page 128.

Parent letter and booklet

It is very important that parents are kept informed about the nature of this new-style homework. Most schools elect to launch IMPACT Shared Writing by having a meeting or a series of meetings. We have included here a draft letter to parents and a booklet which schools may photocopy and give to parents. The booklet is eight A5 pages when copied, folded and collated. This can be given to all new parents as their children start school. There is a space on the cover for the school name.

Keeping shared writing going...

There are a few tips which have been found over the years to make life simpler for parents, teachers and children:

• Don't send shared writing activities in the first few weeks of the September term. Shared writing, like IMPACT maths, usually starts in the third week of the new school year.

• Don't send shared writing activities in the second half of the summer term. Shared writing, like IMPACT maths, usually belongs to the heart of the school year.

• Do value the work that the children and their parents do at home. Sometimes it may not be presented as you expect – for example, a lot of parents with young children write in upper case rather than lower case letters or will ask children to **write over** a line of print. Remember that what comes back into class is a starting point for work that you consider appropriate, and is facilitating both discussion and partnership.

Dear Parents,

In our class, we have decided to use a new 'shared homework scheme' designed to help develop and improve children's writing skills. This will involve sending home a regular task in the form of an A4 sheet. The sheet will outline a simple writing activity for you and your child to enjoy together. These are designed to be shared; the children are not expected to complete the tasks alone.

We would very much like to talk to you about this scheme, and so on _____ we shall hold three short meetings. You need only come to **one** of these and can choose the time which is most convenient:

• 9.00 in the morning
• 3.30 in the afternoon
• 7.00 in the evening.

We would really like as many parents as possible to attend.

Your help in supporting your child's learning is a crucial part of his/her success at school. We do appreciate the time and trouble that parents take with their children, and we can certainly see the benefits in the quality of the children's work and the enthusiasm with which they attack it.

Please return the slip at the bottom of the letter.

Yours sincerely,

_____

Name _____   Class _____

I would like to attend the meeting at:

9.00 in the morning

3.30 in the afternoon

7.00 in the evening

Please tick **one** time only.

Don't forget...

Pick your time!
When you both want
to do the activity.

Don't over-correct!
This can be very
discouraging.

**Your child does not always
have to do all the writing!**
You may take turns, or take
over sometimes.

Make it fun!
If either of you gets tired
or bored help a bit more.
Tasks should not last more
than 20 minutes unless you
want them to!

**Praise and encourage as
much as you can!**

IMPACT

Shared Writing

SPIKE

School name

_____

About Shared Writing

The teacher selects an activity.

The teacher explains the activity to the class.

Child and helper read through the activity.

Child and helper talk about the activity.

Child and helper share the writing.

Child and helper comment on the activity in the diary.

Child brings the activity back into school.

Teacher reads the comments in the diary.

The teacher follows up the activity in class.

Spelling and punctuation

We all agree that correct spelling and punctuation are very important. However........

DO

• Notice punctuation when sharing the writing activity.
• Talk about different uses of capital and lower case letters.
• Play word games such as 'I spy' or 'Hangman'.
• Read what the child has written before you make any comment about spelling, punctuation or presentation.
• Help them learn any words sent home by the school.

DON'T

• Worry about every mistake – children can become very anxious about their writing if constantly interrupted.
• With young children don't insist that they spell every word correctly. At this stage we are encouraging them to 'be writers'.
• Don't worry if your child is quite slow to learn to spell and punctuate – these things come with time and encouragement.

How we write

Writing also has a mechanical side, children have to learn to form their letters, to separate words, to begin and end sentences.

When children are first learning to write it can be very discouraging to be constantly corrected. However, as they become more confident, we can afford to draw their attention to these things:

Starting school

Your child already knows quite a lot about writing when they start........

They may

• be able to tell the difference between writing and pictures;

• realise that writing has words and spaces;

• know some letters of their name;

• be able to make marks on paper or form a few letters;

• understand that 'talk' can be written down and that writing can give messages or information;

• know that we write from left to right in English;

• play at 'reading' their own 'writing'.

Being a writer...

Is about...
Having ideas
Composing them
Communicating them

WANTED
A Purpose
a.k.a.
A Greeting
A Compliment
An Enquiry
A Gossip
A Thought.

To
An Audience
My teacher
Mum or Dad
Friend or foe
Near or far

Choose from our
catalogue of
Types of Writing

a letter
a poster
a list
a book

Parents can help by...

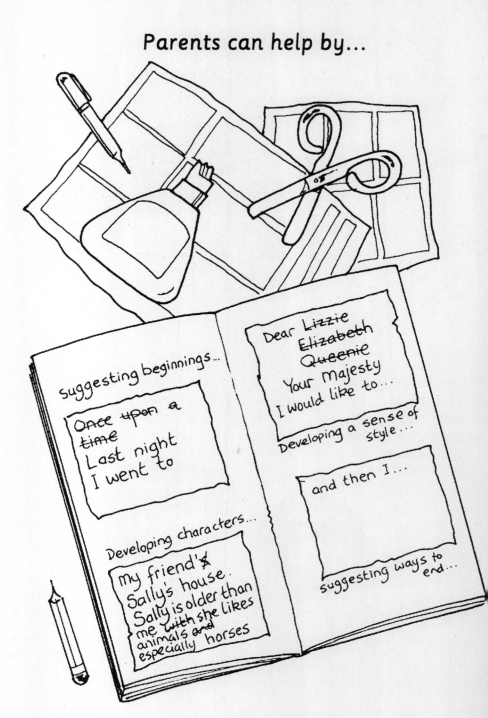

Teachers' Notes
RECEPTION

Where the Wild Things Are Read the book again to remind the children of Max's story. Talk about the kinds of places they have drawn, and ask them to imagine how they have got there. What kind of creatures live in that place; are there monsters like the ones that Max finds? The children could tell their story by drawing two or three pictures (divide up the page for them) telling how they have got to their imaginary, or real, place.
Where the Wild Things Are, Maurice Sendak (Picture Lions)

I'm coming to get you! Display the pictures and talk about the names the children have given to their monsters. How have they written their names? How did they know which letters to use (especially if they are invented spellings)? Invent a new name together; emphasising that this is a new word, and that means that you can decide how it is spelled as long as someone else would be able to read it. Make your own versions of *I'm coming to get you!* based on the format of the Tony Ross book.
I'm coming to get you, Tony Ross (Penguin)

Bear hunt! Display the scary animal pictures, and think of the kind of thing you might say when you finally stumbled across your animal... 'Two black leathery wings, one tiny nose, two big ears, and upside-down... it's a bat!' You can now use the children's ideas in short plays; pool all the best ideas into a class version of *We're going on a bear hunt!*, complete with actions that you could use in an assembly or short presentation to another class.
We're going on a bear hunt, Michael Rosen (Walker Books)

Party preparations You could use these lists to prepare for a small party; for example, to celebrate the school's birthday, Christmas, or another festival. Perhaps you could invite the school caretaker, or the parents who come in to help in school to be the guests. Preparations could include writing the invitations, decorating the class, buying and preparing the food and then holding the party itself.

Cartoon creator Display the pictures of the cartoon characters, and draw attention to the names the children have invented for their characters. How do the names reflect the type of character they are? Choose a few of the characters, and discuss what they do, and the kinds of adventures they might have. Get the children to make up their own stories around their characters; perhaps you could provide them with a page divided into four boxes so they could draw their stories in the style of a comic. They will need you to write captions.

The barking cat You can use the pictures and writing that comes back to the classroom to look at the ways the children have used their knowledge of letters and the sounds they make to construct words; or you can use their mixed-up animals for a fun drama session, where the children have to guess the mixture of animals that each child has chosen.

Best outfit Talk about the pictures the children have brought back. Are there any items of clothing that seem to be everyone's favourites? You could construct a 'washing line' of pictures to display the range of different clothing that the children choose. This information can then be incorporated into any maths data collecting you have started with the children.

Name changing Has anyone named themselves after anyone famous? Try playing a few games where the children have to try and remember their new names! Draw on this the next time you are writing a story all together, and you are trying to think of a suitable name for a character. Remind the children that names are very important in giving us the first idea of what a character might be like.

Whoops! Collect the different stories together into a classbook and read them to the children at storytime, trying to tell the story in as animated a way as possible.

Incy Wincy Spider... You should gather quite a collection of adjectives and describing phrases that apply to very small creatures. You could display these words alongside pictures that the children have drawn of their very small creatures, so they can find their picture, and read their words to the other children in the class. This could also feed into drama work, with the children miming their animal, and then saying their three describing words. The other children can then guess what the animal is.

Nellie the Elephant... You could display the children's words alongside their pictures of their very large creatures, so they can find their picture, and read their words to the other children in the class. This could also feed into drama work, with the children miming their animal, and then saying their three describing words. The other children can then guess what the animal is.

I can sing a rainbow... This work lends itself very well to both art work and some early data handling work. Display the pictures of objects in the favourite colours (paint them bigger and brighter in class if necessary). Give the names of the different colours alongside the pictures – maybe written in the appropriate colours. The children can then use the displays to refer to when they are doing their data handling work; sorting and counting the different children who like the different colours, maybe trying a bar chart or pictogram.

10, 9, 8, 7... You can use the numbered T-shirts that come back to the classroom for a very useful long-term display. There may be some numbers missing between one and ten, but if you make up the gaps, you can make a very colourful numberline that can be referred to by the children whenever they are doing maths work in the class. Numbers above ten could also be incorporated into a number line or saved and used on the carpet for whole-class number games.

Special letters How many children have chosen their initial letter? Get the children to read out their letter, and the words that they have written down that begin with that letter. Does anyone have the same sound as them? Group the children according to the sounds they have chosen – which group has the most children in it? Display the work sorted into these groups – introduce the children to early alphabetic skills by displaying them along the wall in alphabetical order.

Sea world Display the descriptive words alongside the children's pictures so they can find their picture, and read their words to the other children in the class. This could also feed into drama work, with the children miming their animal, and then saying their three describing words. The other children can then guess what their animal is.

Pussy cat, Pussy cat... Display the children's words and pictures so they can find their picture, and read their words to the other children in the class. Try cat stories such as *My cat likes to hide in boxes* by Eve Sutton and Lynley Dodd (Penguin) and any book in the Mog series, for example *Mog, the forgetful cat* by Judith Kerr (Collins).

Venus visitor Display the children's chosen adjectives alongside pictures that the children have coloured of their Venus visitors, so they can find their picture, and read their words to the other children in the class. You might like to follow up this activity by reading a few alien stories such as *But Martin!* by June Counsel (Picture Corgi) or the *Dr Xargle* series of books by Jeanne Willis and Tony Ross (Red Fox). The children could make alien masks, and imagine what it might be like to be an alien visiting their school!

Home sweet home Display the words and pictures so the children can find their picture, and read their words to the other children in the class. In the classroom the children can build models of their ideal homes out of bricks, LEGO, or junk materials. You can then put on an 'Ideal Home Exhibition' of your own! Perhaps the children could design a simple form of the brochures which estate agents produce, to advertise their own home in the exhibition.

Hide and seek Talk about all the different hiding places with the children. Display their pictures under the different rooms in the house – eg. all those in the kitchen, in the sitting room, in the bathroom, etc. You could make a 'house' on the wall full of hiding places. Discuss the characteristics of good hiding places – eg. they are 'warm', dark, secret.... Make a joint list of adjectives.

Night creatures Collect all the night creatures drawings that the children have brought in and display them. Sort them according to the type of animal; are they bird, rodent, or large animal? Have the children ever seen a fox, badger, hedgehog in their garden? Have they ever seen a bat or owl?

The Loch Ness monster You should get some wonderful pictures coming back into class; all of which can be displayed, or perhaps made into a class Loch Ness

monster book. Collect all the names, and talk about why the children chose those names – did they have any help choosing a name? Has anyone chosen a Scottish name? You could elaborate on the theme of swimming in Loch Ness, by writing a class story which tells of how you happened to be there and what you discovered there.

What kind of monster? Use the monster adjectives as a display with the pictures that the children have drawn of their baby monsters, so they can find their picture, and read their words to the other children in the class. The children could mime their monster while the other children guess what the monster is like.

Unusual pets Display the children's words alongside their pictures of their unusual pets, so they can find their picture, and read their words to the other children in the class. The children could mime their animal, and then say their three describing words. The other children can then guess what their animal is.

If you go down to the woods today... Collect everyone's ideas into a class book that the children can then look through on their own. Each page as you open it would have 'If you go down to the woods today, you're sure of a big surprise...' printed on it, showing each child's 'surprise' on one side, with what they would say when they saw it on the other.

One, two, three, four, five... Make a class book that the children can look at on their own. Each page would have 'One, two, three, four, five, once I caught a fish alive. Six, seven, eight, nine, ten, then I let it go again...' printed on it, showing each child's fish on one side, with what they would say when it bit their finger on the other.

Scary things You should get some wonderful pictures coming back into class, all of which can be displayed, or perhaps

made into a class 'Scary things' book. Talk about words which we use to describe scary things... eg. 'dark', 'big', 'frightening'. Make a list together of all the words you can think of.

Fun all year round! Try sorting the activities suggested into categories; outdoor games, indoor games, quiet activities, noisy activities. Do they involve more than one person at a time, are they expensive, do you need any equipment? Make a book of all of the fun things your class likes to do using the writing and pictures done by the children at home. The children can look at it by themselves or with their friends.

Three legs! Make a display of all the three-legged animal pictures. You could link this with maths work on the number three. Look at the names the children have thought of for their animals, and find out the strategies the children used to get to their spellings of the words – how much did they come up with using their knowledge of sounds?

What a mug! Make a display of everyone's mugs; perhaps you could get a bargain box of blank mugs from somewhere, which the children could then paint their designs on to with ceramic paint. Ask how the children came to their spellings of the words – how much did they come up with using their knowledge of sounds?

Secret wish Read Aladdin, or watch a video of the film before the activity goes home so the children understand what a *magic lamp* is! Display the children's wishes in puffs of smoke coming from a huge lamp on the wall. Read them together, drawing attention to the children's names on each wish. Write stories about finding the magic lamps, and what happened next.

Dreaming Read some stories to the children about dreams, for example Joseph and his coat of many colours from the Bible (which might be a little difficult). You could mount the children's drawings on cloud-

shaped pieces of paper and display them over a picture of someone sleeping.

Little Miss Muffet... Consider all the things that the children have written down which give them a fright. Try using the children's 'frightening thing' to rewrite the Miss Muffet rhyme. For example, 'Little Miss Muffet sat on her tuffet, eating her curds and whey, when down came a snake, and hissed in her ear, and frightened Miss Muffet away!'

Peter Pan Get the children to paint pictures of their crocodile which you can display with the names the children have chosen. You could sort the names into initial letter groups, find out who has the longest name, the shortest name. You could make a book all about the crocodile's adventures.

Slow and **Fast** Make a book of all the slow and fast creatures that the children have drawn pictures of. Talk about them and see if the children know anything about them. Sort the animals into groups; the children could provide the categories. Use information books and research into the animals with the children.

Ladybird, ladybird Display the pictures of ladybirds that the children have done, how many spots have they put on them; are they all red ladybirds? Can the children say the rhyme? Get the children to describe to you what they think the ladybird's house is like. Paint pictures in school of the children's descriptions.

Birthday cake Look at all the pictures of birthday cakes together with the children. Sort them into groups of four candles, and five candles. Can the children think of any other categories we could sort the cakes into? (Eg according to colour, cars, people, monsters etc.) Make small cakes in the classroom that the children can write their initials on in coloured icing. Do any of the children know when their birthday is? Who has a birthday soon?

Where the Wild Things Are

Max was sent to his room without his supper. He went to the land where the Wild Things are.

● Draw a picture of the place you would go, if you could travel to an imaginary land.

● Write your name on your picture.

To the helper:

● What can your child remember about the story?
● If your child wants you to, you could write down the name of their imaginary place for them.

This activity involves your child recalling a specific storybook. In class we shall use their ideas for different scenarios to stimulate creative writing, in response to the original story.

_____and

child

_____

helper(s)

_____

did this activity together

_____and

child

_____

helper(s)

_____

did this activity together

I'm coming to get you!

Tony Ross talks about a scary monster that's coming to get us!

● What sort of monster do you think is coming to get you?

● Draw a picture of it and give it a name.

Bear Hunt!

Michael Rosen writes:

One shiny wet nose,
   Two big goggly eyes...
      ...It's a bear!

● Draw a picture of something you might go on a hunt for.

To the helper:

● What can your child remember about the story?

● Try to think together of an animal that might be scary if you were to bump into it in the dark... e.g. a crocodile, or a panther.

In the book *We're going on a bear hunt*, Michael Rosen has committed to paper a well-known song loved by many children. We shall use the children's ideas to write our own versions of the story back at school.

_____and

child

_____

helper(s)

_____

did this activity together

_____and

child

_____

helper(s)

_____

did this activity together

Party preparations

Pretend you're going to have a party.

● Make a list of all the things you will need to prepare for the party.

● Think about who will come, what food you could have and what games you could play.

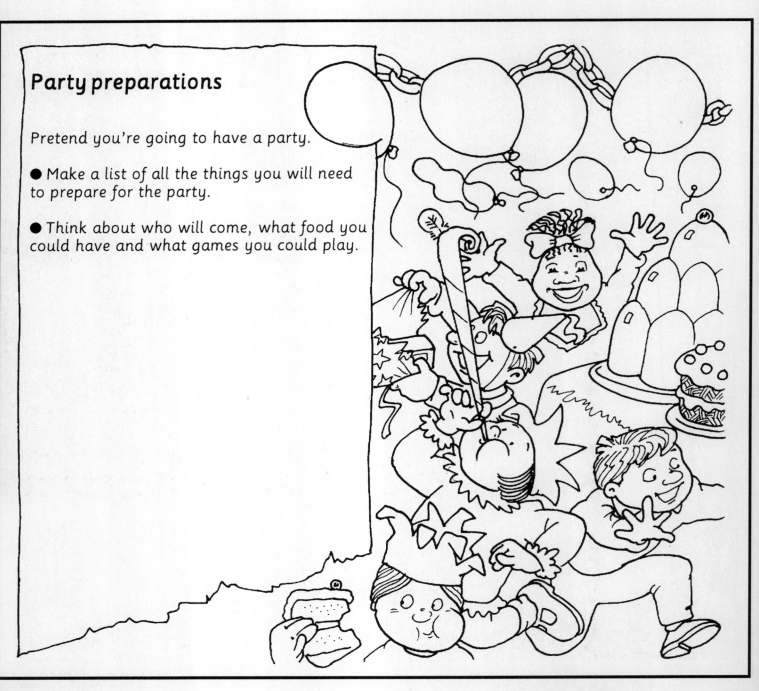

Cartoon creator

● Draw a cartoon character of your own and give it a name.

To the helper:

● Talk about cartoon characters that you both know; like Mickey Mouse, Bugs Bunny or SuperTed. What are these characters like, what do they do?

● Talk about the character they have created, and what is special about him or her.

● Help your child to do any writing, if necessary.

Inventing characters, and names for any kind of character is very important in the process of story writing. We shall use these characters for creating storylines and stories together in the classroom.

_____and

child

_____

helper(s)

_____

did this activity together

_____and

child

_____

helper(s)

_____

did this activity together

The barking cat

● Draw a picture of an animal.

● Give your animal a voice, **but** make it the voice of another animal!

● Make it as funny as you can.

● Write the voice in a speech bubble.

Best outfit

● What is your favourite item of clothing?

● Draw a picture of it and label it with your helper. Tell your helper why you like it.

To the helper:

● Talk about the clothes your child likes to wear, and ask why he or she likes to wear them.

Making lists is an important organisational skill in writing. Back in the classroom we will discuss the information that the children have gathered to talk about how clothes have changed over time. We shall then use our imaginations to write down what the children think we will all be wearing in the future.

_____and

child

_____

helper(s)

_____

did this activity together

_____and

child

_____

helper(s)

_____

did this activity together

Name changing

● What is your name?

● If you could change your name, what would you change it to?

● Choose a name and write it down.
Explain why you chose that name to your helper.

Whoops!

- *Have you ever dropped something that broke?*
- *Draw a picture of what it was that you dropped. Write your name on your picture.*
- *Tell your helper what happened and ask your helper to write it all down in your words.*

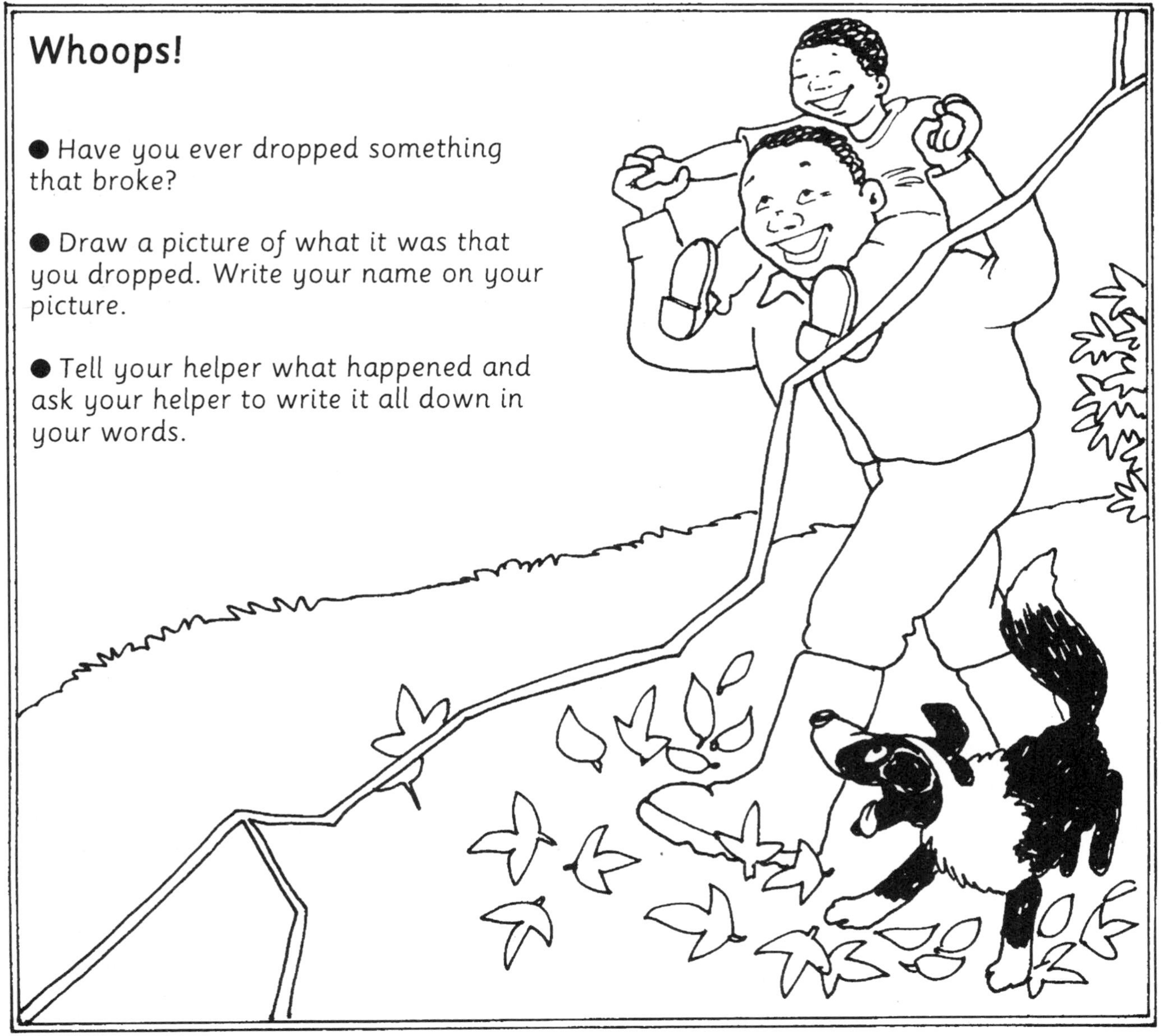

To the helper:

- Talk about their memories of the event; was it something precious that broke?
- Write down what your child says *in their words.*

Anecdotal stories are a hugely important part of storytelling skills. The way these personal stories are told have a particular style and pattern depending on the teller and the listener. It is important that children learn early on that the spoken style can be written down.

____________________ and
child

____
helper(s)

____

did this activity together

_____and

child

_____

helper(s)

_____

did this activity together

Incy Wincy Spider...

● Draw a very small animal.

● Think of three words to describe it. Is it fast, twitchy, soft? Write down the words with your helper.

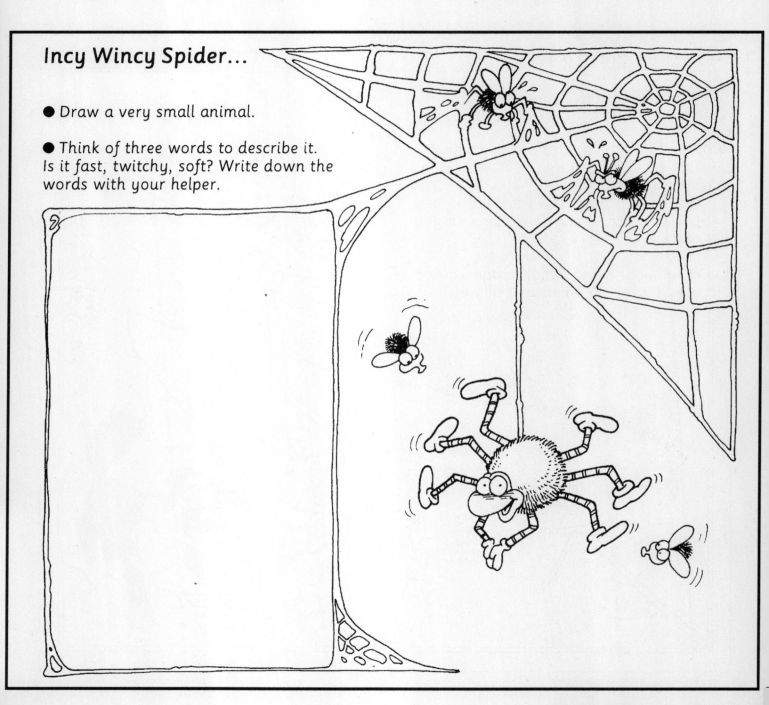

Nellie the elephant...

● Draw a very large animal.

● Think of three words to describe it. Is it slow, heavy or noisy? Write down the words with your helper.

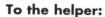
_____and

child

_____

helper(s)

_____

did this activity together

_____and

child

_____

helper(s)

_____

did this activity together

I can sing a rainbow...

● What is your favourite colour?
Try and write the word.

● Draw something that is that colour.

10, 9, 8, 7,...

● What is your favourite number?
Write the number and then try
and write the word
(for example, **5** and *five*).

● Draw a T-shirt with that number on it.

To the helper:

● Talk about your
favourite number, and
why it is your favourite.
● Think about the sounds
in the word; try to get your
child to guess at least the
first letter in the word.

**Knowing and being
able to recognise the
different numbers both
numerically and as
words is a very
important skill. This
activity gets the children
talking about numbers,
and provides an
opportunity to consider
how a word is spelled.**

_____and

child

_____

helper(s)

_____

did this activity together

_____and

child

_____

helper(s)

_____

did this activity together

Special letters

● What is your favourite letter? Ask your helper to help you write three words that begin with that letter.

● Draw something that begins with that letter.

impact WRITING HOMEWORK

Sea world

● Draw something that lives in the water.

● Think of three words to describe it. Is it smooth, playful, quick? Ask your helper to write them down.

To the helper:

● Talk about all the sea creatures that you can think of together, and then choose one that you like the best.
● Think about the sounds in the words; try to get your child to guess at least the first letters.

This activity encourages the children to use new adjectives. We shall compare all the wonderful words that the children think of back in the classroom.

_____and

child

_____

helper(s)

_____

did this activity together

_____and

child

_____

helper(s)

_____

did this activity together

Pussy cat, Pussy cat...

This is Oz.
He is a large stripey tabby cat.

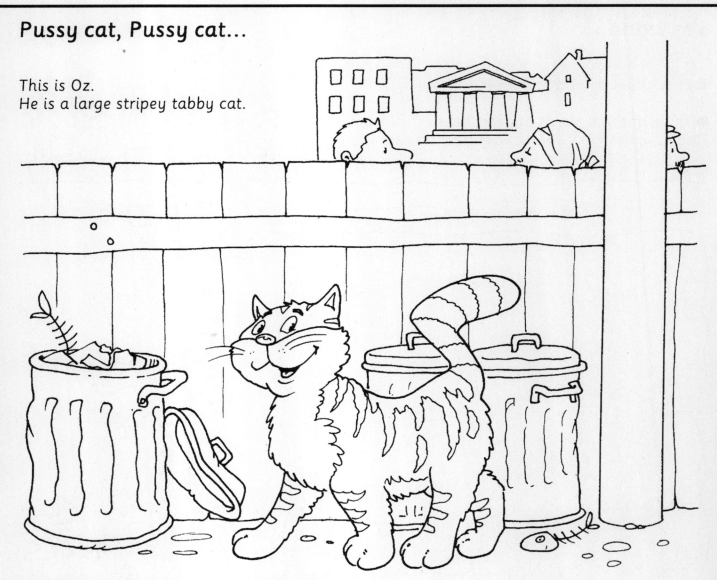

● Think of three words to describe his character. Can you write them down with your helper?

Perhaps he is like a cat you know?

Venus visitor

This is a space monster from Venus.

● Think of three words to describe his character. Write them down, with your helper.

● Colour him in.

_____and

child

_____

helper(s)

_____

did this activity together

_____and

child

_____

helper(s)

_____

did this activity together

Home sweet home

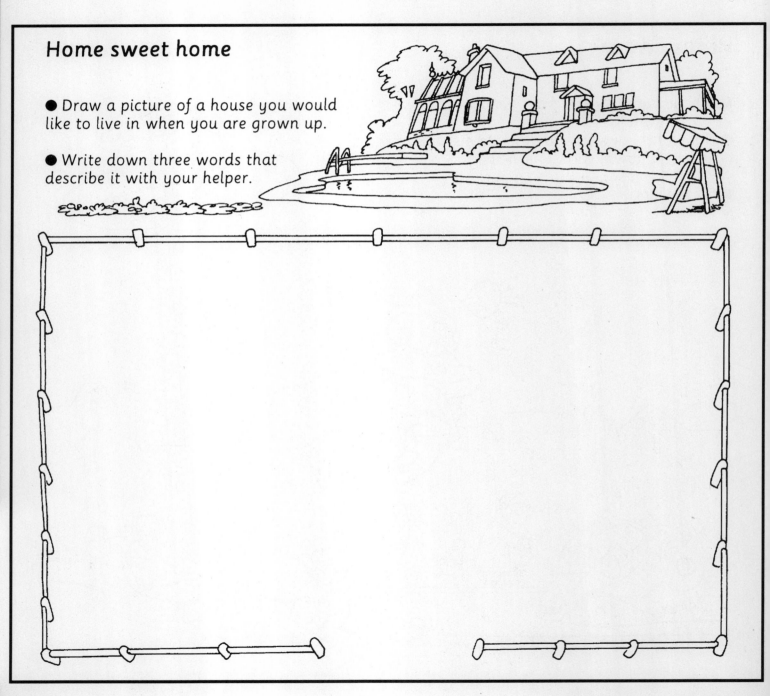

● Draw a picture of a house you would like to live in when you are grown up.

● Write down three words that describe it with your helper.

impact WRITING HOMEWORK

Hide and seek

- Where in your home is a good place to hide?

- Ask your helper to help you look for one...

- Write down where it is.

- Draw yourself hiding there.

To the helper:

- Have a hunt around the house for the best (and safest!) place to hide – perhaps you could play a game of hide and seek together.
- Think about the sounds in the words; try to get your child to guess at least the first letters.

Through having to write down the place where they like to hide, the children are having to concentrate on the sounds in the words, and think of the letters that make those sounds. We shall talk about favourite hiding places back at school.

_____and

child

_____

helper(s)

_____

did this activity together

impact WRITING HOMEWORK

_____and

child

_____

helper(s)

_____

did this activity together

Night creatures

Imagine that you are outside in the middle of the night.

● Draw an animal or bird you might see.

● Write down its name.

impact WRITING HOMEWORK

The Loch Ness monster

Imagine that you are swimming in Loch Ness.

● Draw the monster you meet!

● Write down its name.

_____and

child

_____

helper(s)

_____

did this activity together

_____and

child

_____

helper(s)

_____

did this activity together

What kind of monster?

● Draw a baby monster.

● Think of three words to describe him or her. Write them down with your helper.

impact WRITING HOMEWOR

Unusual pets

Imagine an unusual pet.

● Draw it. Write a few words to describe it.

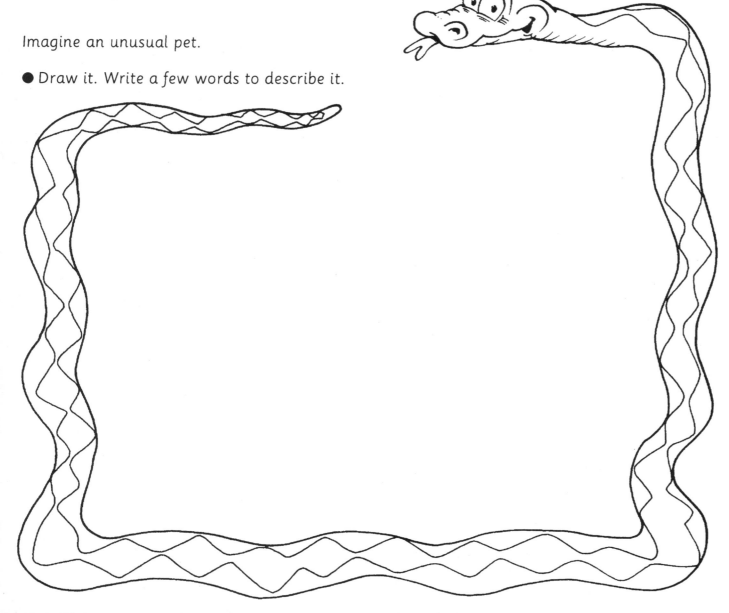

To the helper:

● Think of strange pets you, for example a snake, a giraffe, or an earwig!

● Chose your strange animal, and brainstorm as many words as you can to describe it; for example, very tall, hungry, or slimy. Write down one of the descriptions.

● Think about the sounds in the words; try to get your child to guess at least the first letters.

This encourages the children to use unfamiliar adjectives and gives your child a chance to relate the letter sound to the actual letter. Back in class we shall talk about the descriptive words that they have devised.

_____and

child

_____

helper(s)

_____

did this activity together

_____and

child

_____

helper(s)

_____

did this activity together

If you go down to the woods today...

If you go down to the woods today, you're sure of a big surprise...

● Draw the surprise.

● Write down what you would say when you saw it!

impact WRITING HOMEWOR

One, two, three, four, five once I caught a fish alive...

Six seven eight nine ten, then I let it go again.

● Draw the fish which you caught.

● Write down what you said when it bit your finger!

To the helper:

● Sing the rhyme together first.
● Think about the sounds in the words; try to get your child to guess at least the first letters.

The children are learning here how to write down <u>sounds</u>, and they are finding out that sounds can be represented by writing.

_____and

child

_____

helper(s)

_____

did this activity together

_____and

child

_____

helper(s)

_____

did this activity together

Scary things

● What things are you scared of?

● Draw something you think is scary!

● Write down what it is.

Fun all year round!

● What is a fun game to play in the summer or the winter?

● Draw yourself doing it.

● Write down what you are doing.

To the helper:

● Have a good think about the best games to play. Perhaps you could play one of the games together.

● Think about the sounds in the words; try to get your child to guess at least the first letters.

Through having to write down the names of their favourite games, the children are having to concentrate on the sounds in the words, and think of the letters that make those sounds. We shall talk about favourite games back at school.

_____and

child

_____

helper(s)

_____

did this activity together

_____and

child

_____

helper(s)

_____

did this activity together

Three legs!

- Make up an animal with three legs!

- Draw a picture of it, and give it a name.

- Write down its name.

What a mug!

- Design a mug.

- Draw a picture to go on the mug, and some words, or a word to go with it.

Perhaps your mug is for someone special, or for a special occasion like a birthday, or Mother's Day.

To the helper:

- Have you got any mugs with pictures or writing on them? Have a look at them for inspiration; what sort of thing do they have written on them? Perhaps they are mugs that have been souvenirs, or presents; do any of your mugs have jokes on them?

Through having to write something on their mug, the children are having to concentrate on the sounds in the words, and think of the letters that make those sounds. We shall look at all of the mug designs when we get them back to school.

_____and

child

_____

helper(s)

_____

did this activity together

_____and

child

_____

helper(s)

_____

did this activity together

Secret wish

You have been given a magic lamp which, when you rub it, produces a magic Genie that can grant wishes!

● What would you wish for?

● Draw a picture of what you would wish for, and ask your helper to write down your wish.

● Write your name on your picture.

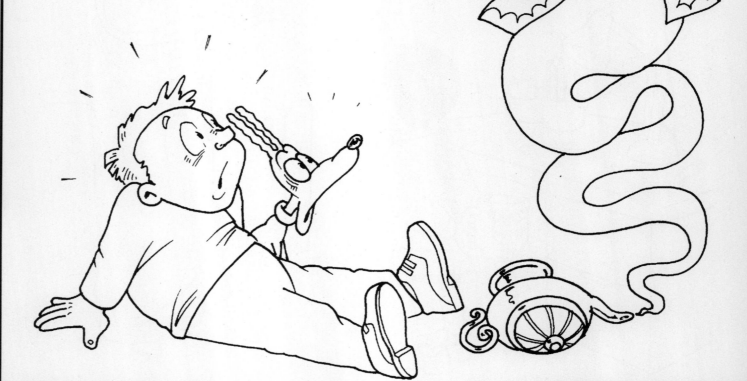

Dreaming

- Have you every had a funny dream?

- Draw a picture of a dream you remember.

- Write a few words about it with your helper.

To the helper:

- Talk about the dreams your children (or you) have had. Do you recall any funny ones?
- Try doing the writing together – talk about the sounds and letters in the words, and get your child to provide as much of the information as he/she can. For example, what sounds can you hear in that word? What is the first sound – can you write that one down?
- Take over with the parts that you can do, but your child cannot manage yet.

We shall make up dream stories and share these back in the classroom. We will also illustrate our dreams.

_____and

child

_____

helper(s)

_____

did this activity together

_____and

child

_____

helper(s)

_____

did this activity together

Little Miss Muffet...

Little Miss Muffet sat on her tuffet,
Eating her curds and whey,
When down came a spider,
And sat down beside her,
And frightened Miss Muffet away!

Perhaps spiders don't frighten you.

● What could come and sit next to you that would frighten you away?

● Draw a picture and write its name.

Peter Pan

The story of Peter Pan tells us how everyone could always hear the crocodile coming because he had swallowed a clock.

● What would be a good name for the crocodile? Try and write it down.

● Draw a picture of your crocodile.

To the helper:

● Talk about the story of Peter Pan – how much of the story can you remember together?

● You can make up a name, or use a real one; but try to follow your child's lead in the spelling of it – get them to try and work out what the letters should be from their sounds.

We shall have great fun back in the classroom sharing everyone's crocodile names, and we will write our own adventures for the crocodile, using the well-known story as a stimulus.

_____and

child

_____

helper(s)

_____

did this activity together

_____and

child

_____

helper(s)

_____

did this activity together

Slow

● Which animals can you think of that move slowly?

● Draw a picture of your favourite and write down its name.

Fast

- Which animals can you think of that can move quickly?
- Draw a picture of your favourite and write down its name.

To the helper:

- Talk about all the fast-moving animals that you can think of; for example cheetahs, flies or horses, and choose one that your child would like to draw a picture of.
- Think about the sounds in the words; try to get your child to guess at least the first letters.

Back in the classroom we shall display all the pictures and names of animals which move quickly, and see if we can find out some more information about the animals.

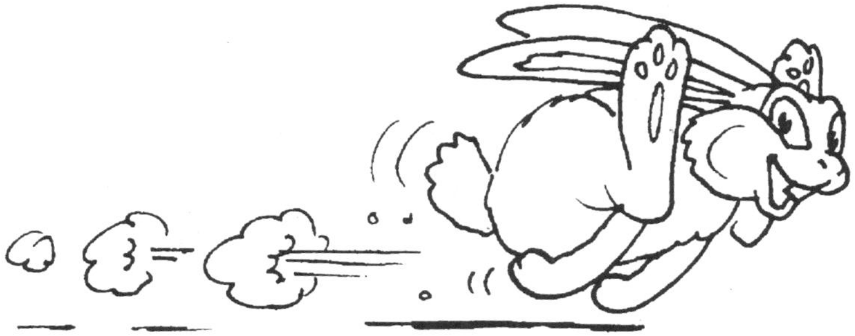

____________________ and
child

____
helper(s)

____
did this activity together

_____and

child

_____

helper(s)

_____

did this activity together

Ladybird, Ladybird fly away home...

● Draw a big picture of a ladybird.

● What do you think its home looks like? Describe what you think it looks like, and get your helper to write it down.

● Draw a picture of its home if you have time.

Birthday cake

● What sort of cake would you like for your birthday?

● What shape would it be? Draw a picture – don't forget to put the right number of candles on your cake!

● Write your name beside the cake.

To the helper:

● Talk about the best birthday cakes you have seen; and emphasise that this is not necessarily the cake they *will* get on their birthday, it's just pretend!

Back in the classroom the children will sort their birthday cakes into ages – who is 5 already, and who is still 4. We will also talk about why the children have chosen the designs they have.

_____and

child

_____

helper(s)

_____

did this activity together

Teachers' Notes
YEAR ONE

Titles Let each child choose a book to take home for this activity. Afterwards, get the children to rewrite their titles in large, colourful letters so you can display them in the book corner. Can the children recognise which title belongs to which book? Encourage the children to talk about their books – would they recommend them to other children?

The Owl and the Pussycat Read through the whole poem in the classroom. Talk about the nonsense, or unusual words – why did Edward Lear use them in his poem? Read some more Edward Lear with the children and see if they can spot the nonsense words again. Try writing your own short nonsense poems (an easy way to start this off is by changing the words in a well known nursery rhyme or song).

International stories Read the stories out to the rest of the class, and explain where they come from. The next time you write stories, refer back to the style 'captured' in these stories. Start by asking them to say the first few lines as if they were going to tell the story orally. That should be what they write down.

Favourite page Display the pictures from the favourite pages in the book corner, or near where you keep the books. Can the children recognise which pictures belong to which book? Get the children talking about their books – ask them if they would recommend them to other children.

Fairy tale count-up! Sort the characters the children have thought of into categories – good, evil, beautiful, ugly. Next, brainstorm all the places an adventure could happen (real-life or magical). Finally, list all the strange or magical objects that appear in stories (such as magic lamps, magic keys, mysterious packages etc). Write all these words – characters; places; objects – on card and create three story bags. When the children next write a story, they can take up to three characters from the character bag, and then one from each of the other bags; and they must do their best to write a story that includes all of the elements they have picked out of the bags.

Film characters/Funny film Display the pictures of the characters, and draw attention to the names they have invented for their characters. How do they reflect the type of character they are? Get the children to write their own stories around their characters. Provide the children with a page divided into four boxes so they could write their stories in the style of a comic.

Fill the gaps Have some book titles with the words missing for the children to fill in in class eg. *The Very Wobbly Caterpillar, I want my banana*. Make a list of funny names to replace our own names beginning with the same letter – eg. 'Thomas' becomes *tadpole* and 'Amy' becomes *anteater*. This is good for reinforcing initial sounds!

Sheep-pig Display the pictures the children have brought in of their strange animals; can the children guess what they are called from their pictures? Read the children (or tell them) the story of the *Sheep-pig* by Dick King-Smith (Penguin) and then ask them to make up their own strange animal stories using their animal inventions.

Children's rhymes/Vehicle rhymes Are there any rhymes that are new to the other children? Perhaps you could learn them together. Write out the words to the songs on a large sheet of paper so all the

children can see the words. Each time you sing it you could appoint one of the better readers to be a *pointer* to keep track of where you are in the song.

Party, party! You could really have some fun following up this activity! When the lists of party foods come in, ask if the children can guess the character from the food they would have at their party? Using junk, or Plasticine or clay and a paper plate, the children could then make a plate of food for their character, and put it in a display next to a large picture of them. You could even take this further, by writing invitations to guests they might invite. Can they imagine what might happen at the party?

Rosie's walk Read *Rosie's Walk* by Pat Hutchins (Penguin) in class before you send this activity home. Write a class book of Rosie's walk, but fill in the story on the Wolf's side of the page telling his side of the story; with this thoughts, and anything he might be saying written down. Talk about the importance of pictures in a story, and how they can sometimes tell a completely different story to the one in the text. Are there any books you know of that do not have any words at all? Try letting the children take over at storytime with 'wordless' books.

Happy families! Read some of the *Happy Families* books in class (Allan Ahlberg, Penguin). Get the children to write their own Happy Family story books, using the characters they have created. Talk through a few of the 'Families' and their possible adventures with the children to give them a few ideas. Provide each child with a little book made from folded sheets of A4 paper – about the size of the original Happy Family books.

Fairy tale brainstorm! Make a big list of all the words the children have thought of; try to sort them into categories – characters, places, magical objects, places, times. Now write out cards as for **Fairy tale count-up!**

Design a drink You can make a great 3[ ] wall display from the work produced by thi[ ] activity. Talk about the names of drinks they have thought of, and what kinds of drink they are; sort them into categories (citrus fruit, tropical fruit, new flavours, cola drinks etc). Now you can roll card into can-size tubes to show the children what the cans will look like, and then give the card to them flat. The children now have to use thei[ ] designs that they did at home to help them finish their cans. Look at a few real cans to help the children remember the kind of information you see on a can. You can now staple or pin these 'cans' on the wall, rolled into their intended shape!

Postcard from the moon This activity will fit in well with any work to do with either letter-writing, space or holidays. To display both sides at once place the postcards into clear plastic files. The children can then flick through the file and look at both sides of the cards.

The trouble with... Before sending this activity home, read some of the *The Trouble with...* series by Babette Cole (Armada Picture Lions) with the children. Collect up a[ ] the *The trouble with...* sentences, and read some through with the children; can anyone guess from what has been written who the author is? Get the children to work in pairs to talk about their stories, and develop them a bit further before writing them down (limit the time on this part to about five minutes).

Not now, Bernard Before sending this activity home, make sure you read *Not now, Bernard* by David McKee (Sparrow Books) at least once. Afterwards collect all the comic strips together, and talk about the different ways the children have divided up the story. These can then be displayed on a wall or in a class book. If children are having difficulty planning their stories, this method of quickly sketching an outline in three or four consecutive boxes can help considerably.

Leaving home How did the children organise their lists? Has anyone drawn a picture of their bag with all their things in it? Write stories about children who decide to leave home; why have they left? What did they take? What happened to them?

School likes and dislikes Talk about the kinds of things that are popular or unpopular at school. Sort them. Try writing some letters to the school governors explaining the good and bad points of the school as seen by the children in this class. Make some suggestions for improvements, ask questions, and maybe even invite a governor into the class to discuss the issues raised by the activity.

Call 999! Discuss the types of questions the children would be asked if they had to dial 999. Invite someone from the Emergency services – perhaps a parent – to come and talk about how real life can be quite different from what they see on the television. Get the children to plan a short play, incorporating what they would say if that emergency was real. This work would fit in well with a topic on *People who help us*. Also, it will give you another opportunity to make sure the children can say their own address and telephone number.

The day I fell over! This work can be used in drama work, or it can be used as a starting point for some written work. Pair up the children, and get them to take turns being the reporter, who must listen carefully to the other child, and take notes. (These could be letters or pictures – anything that will help them remember.) Then they swap over. The children can write up their own notes or dictate to an adult.

Advice to an old woman This is a nice activity to do just before or after the holidays. Once you have collected all the children's ideas together, you could print them up in the form of a *holiday ideas* booklet which can then go home with the children in the holidays.

When I grow up... Discuss the children's ambitions and ideas with them. Talk about their reasons – why do they want to be a footballer or a brain surgeon? Talk about jobs and earning a living. The children can think about what a day in the life of a person doing their chosen occupation would be like. Can they write a few sentences entitled 'A day in the life of a...'?

Teddy bear's picnic Make a display in class of all the things that the children have drawn pictures of; showing the teddy bears all sitting together, with their basket unpacked and the food out to see. Discuss what happens on picnics. Has anyone been on a picnic where it rained? Where it was muddy? Perhaps they can write about a picnic they have been on.

Puppet presenter Let everyone say what their presenter's name is, and what they do. You could try making the puppets from junk materials (eg paper bags, old socks, boxes etc). Perhaps the children could animate their puppets and think up short skits for them – you can make televisions for the children out of a cardboard box!

Shopping lists Get the children to read out their lists to one another in the classroom; can the other children guess their character from the list? What do the shopping lists say about the characters that a story does not; have the children filled in any details that the creators of the characters did not include?

Door plate The children's signs will make a wonderful display. Make a list of the words used. Which signs do the children think are the funniest? Talk about other sorts of signs that we see on doors. Can they find some examples?

Badges! Try sorting them into categories; funny, serious, charity, special days etc. Why have the children chosen their messages? Do they have any connections at home with, for example, a specific charity that their parents support? Display

the badges or use safety pins to attach them to a coat or scarf!

T-shirt Try sorting the designs into categories; funny, serious, charity, special days etc. Why have the children chosen their messages? Display their designs on a washing line around the class. You may be able to get hold of some very cheap T-shirts that the children can write their own designs on – you can use either fabric paint/pens.

Horses for courses Share all the animals and names that the children have thought of. Who has thought of the most unusual pet? Has anyone used the name from a famous animal or pet? Can they tell the story that they took it from? Sort the animals that the children have drawn pictures of into groups. Display the pictures and names in a book of *Peculiar pets*. You could expand this by researching into what kind of food, accommodation, and care each animal would need, and include it in the book.

What a shock! Accumulate everyone's 'shocks' into one book or poem. You could write a basic frame that would repeat every few lines, into which you could fit the children's own experiences. For example 'I was just... when... What a shock I got!' Once you have stuck in their illustrations, and you have read it through with the children, they will then be able to go back to it on their own and read it for themselves.

Rainbow's end Paint the end of a huge rainbow under which the children can display their treasures. Write a class story together telling of how one person (create a character, or choose a child from the class) came to find treasure at the end of the rainbow. Then get the children to write their own stories, using themselves as the main character, and using their ideas for the treasure. This work would fit in very well with any class work about the weather.

A new ride at the fair Talk about everyone's ideas for names for the roundabout, and their pictures of their favourite rides. Use the children's ideas to plan a class fair. Stick a few large sheets of paper together, and get the children to draw on their favourite rides in the places they think they should go.

Animal crackers! Get the children to hold up pictures of their animal crackers, and retell their stories (you could spread these out over the day, or have a few children tell their stories at each storytime.) Get the children to think about what was so funny in each instance. Read some funny animal stories with the children.

Horrid cake Read the children *The toy's party* by Roderick Hunt (Oxford Reading Tree OUP) in which the main character, Kipper, makes a horrid cake for his toys because he doesn't know how to make a real cake. Get the children to write their own horrid cake stories. Make real cakes in the class; what are the things that go into a cake that make it taste nice?

Animal nanny Before you send this activity home, make sure the children understand the role of the dog in the Darling family in the Peter Pan story. This story lends itself to so much creative and imaginative work: making models of Never Never Land; imagining what it would be like to fly; writing short descriptive pieces of writing about this; imagining their own narrow escape from Captain Hook or the crocodile. Peter Pan never wanted to grow up; what do the children want to be when they grow up? What is good about being a child, and what is good about being a grown-up?

_____and

child

_____

helper(s)

_____

did this activity together

Titles

● What is the name of the book you have brought home?

● Write it down. This is its title.

● Can you think of a better one?

● Write that one down, too.

The Owl and the Pussycat

● Say the rhyme of **The Owl and the Pussycat** to your helper.

● What beautiful but strange language! Write down your favourite line and draw a picture of the scene it describes.

● Which words do you think are made up?

To the helper:

● Some of the words in this poem are very strange, but very interesting. What do you think a Runcible Spoon is, for example? Have a few guesses; perhaps you could find out together what they are (if they are real!)

● Help with the spelling if necessary.

This activity will encourage the children to look very closely at a nonsense poem, which will help them when reading or writing nonsense poetry in the classroom.

_____and

child

_____

helper(s)

_____

did this activity together

_____and

child

_____

helper(s)

_____

did this activity together

International stories

● Do you know a story from a different country? Tell the story to your helper; or perhaps your helper knows one to tell you.

Your helper could write down your story.

● Write down the title of the story, and then draw three pictures that tell the story.

● Can anyone you know write a story from another country in that country's language? (Or maybe just the title.)

Favourite page

● What is your favourite page from the book you have taken home?

● What happened on that page?

● Write down what happened on that page in your own words.

Perhaps you could do a picture to go with your writing.

To the helper:

● Help with the writing if necessary.
● Talk about what is happening on that page and in the rest of the book.

Writing and drawing helps the child respond to the story by interpreting it in their own words and images.

_____ and

child

_____

helper(s)

_____

did this activity together

_____and

child

_____

helper(s)

_____

did this activity together

Fairy tale count-up!

● Write down three people or creatures that you think are important in a fairy tale. You might think of a wicked witch, a princess or a dragon.

● Bring your list into school.

● Discuss whether your characters are good or evil?

impact WRITING HOMEWOR

Film characters

Imagine you are going to make a film!

It is a cartoon.

● Write down the names of three characters you will have in your cartoon.

● Draw a picture of them if you can!

● What sort of things will they get up to?

● Tell your helper the story of your film.

To the helper:

● Talk about the sounds in the names of the cartoon characters, and give some help with the writing (if necessary).

● Your child might want you to write down their story – you could be their secretary, and then the story can be shared at school.

This activity will help the children with their storytelling skills. We will share their stories in the classroom.

_____and

child

_____

helper(s)

_____

did this activity together

_____and

child

_____

helper(s)

_____

did this activity together

Funny film

Imagine you are going to make a film!

It is a funny film. You want to make everyone laugh!

● Write down the names of two characters you will have in your film.

● Draw a picture of them.

● Describe where the story takes place. Can you draw the place?

Fill the gaps

● Write down the titles of some of your books.

● Remove one word!

● Replace that word with a different word or even with more than one word.

Try to make the titles as funny as possible!

For example, We're going on a **bun** hunt!
The **clockword mouse** came to tea.

To the helper:

● Try doing this together on a few books – take it in turns. Who can make the funniest title?

This provides an opportunity to talk about what kind of words can replace other words and what kind of words can't. So children can see that a *naming word* or noun must be replaced by another *naming word* for the sentence to make sense.

_____and

child

_____

helper(s)

_____

did this activity together

_____and

child

_____

helper(s)

_____

did this activity together

Sheep-pig

(with apologies to Dick King-Smith)

● Make up an animal like this:
• Sheep-pig
• Duck-dog

● Draw a picture of your animal and write its name down.

Children's rhymes

● Can you think of any nursery rhymes or songs with children in them?

● Write down a list of their titles.

To the helper:

● This activity will require a certain amount of time for remembering, singing, and saying songs and rhymes. You may find that you need to ask other people in your house for help.

Writing lists is an important skill. It is a quick way of collecting and sorting ideas. We shall be singing the songs back in the classroom.

_____and

child

_____

helper(s)

_____

did this activity together

_____and

child

_____

helper(s)

_____

did this activity together

Vehicle rhymes

● Can you think of any nursery rhymes or songs with vehicles in them?

● Write down a list of their titles.

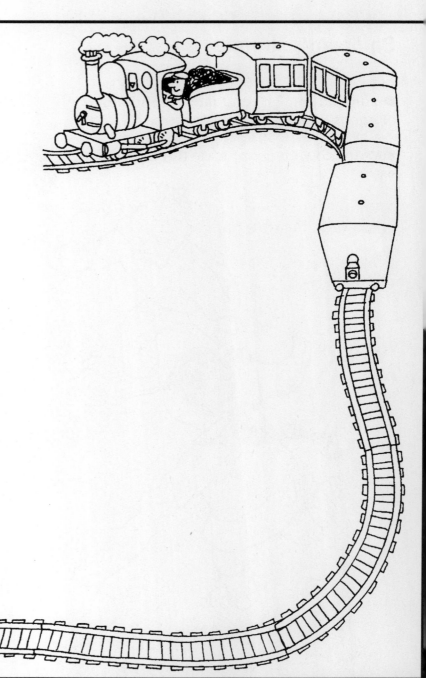

Party, party!

- Who is the main character in the story you are reading?

Imagine that they are going to have a party.

- What kind of food would they prepare for their friends?

- Write down a list of the foods; you could draw a picture, too!

To the helper:
- Talk about the story your child has brought home. Make sure your child understands what a *main character* is.
- Talk about the main character – is it an animal, monster, person, etc? What kinds of food would they like to eat? What would their friends be like? What kind of food would they eat?
- If the list gets very long, take over with the writing.

Thi encourages the children to concentrate on the personality of a character, to think around that character, and fill in details not necessarily provided by the book.

_____and

child

_____

helper(s)

_____

did this activity together

_____and

child

_____

helper(s)

_____

did this activity together

Rosie's Walk

● Tell the story of **Rosie's Walk** to your helper. How is this book clever? Does the writing say anything about the fox? Write down something you think the fox might be thinking by the end of the story.

● Draw a picture, and write the thoughts in a thought bubble...

● Do you know any other stories that have another storyline running through the illustrations?

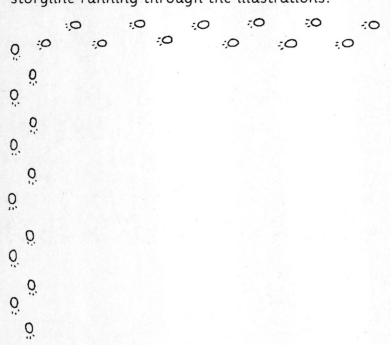

Happy Families!

● Have you ever read any of the **Happy Family** books by the Ahlbergs?

● Tell the story of one you know to your helper.

Think of a new Happy Families character, and then the names for the rest of their family.

● Write down their names and draw pictures of them all.

● Tell your helper what they get up to in your story.

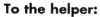

To the helper:

● Talk about your Happy Family characters, and the effect of their jobs on the rest of the family. How do the stories resolve themselves?
● Think of a good job for mum or dad, which you could build a story around (for example, a lion tamer).
● If your child wants, you could write down what happens in your story.

Reading and talking about these books gives an idea of the author's style and purpose. It gives children a framework for their own ideas. We shall be using the ideas you come up with to write our own 'Happy Family' books at school.

_____and

child

_____

helper(s)

_____

did this activity together

_____and

child

_____

helper(s)

_____

did this activity together

Fairy tale brainstorm!

● Work together with a helper to write down as many words as you can to do with fairy tales.

Remember – brainstorming means that **any** words you think of are acceptable.

Design a drink

● What are the names of your favourite drinks?
Think of a name for a new drink.

● Draw its can or bottle.

To the helper:

● What are the drinks that your child chooses to drink at home? If they see a new drink advertised on the TV do they want to try it?
● Look at the designs on drinks you have at home. What colours are used, can you describe the style of writing on them? What about advertising slogans?
● Give a hand with spelling and writing.

Product name and design are vital in deciding a product's success. Creating a new drink name draws on the children's creative abilities, by getting them to design a product they imagine other children might buy.

_____and

child

_____

helper(s)

_____

did this activity together

_____and

child

_____

helper(s)

_____

did this activity together

Postcard from the moon

Imagine that you are on the moon.

● Write a postcard to someone at home, telling them all about it.

You could draw a picture of a scene from the moon on one side, and write your message and your address on the other just like a real postcard!

The trouble with...

- The trouble with my Mum/Dad is...

- The trouble with Me is...

Finish these sentences with your helper.

To the helper:

- The Babette Cole books *The Trouble with Mum, The Trouble with Uncle etc..* have a wonderful twist in the tail. The story is told from the child's point of view, and each concern an odd relative. Think of some strange things that you or your child could be (eg a Superhero).
- Think of what to write together, and let your child write it down. Give them a hand if necessary.

These are a kind of 'Story start'; an alternative to 'Once upon a time...' We shall be reading the books, talking about the ideas we had and then writing our own 'The trouble with...' stories.

_____and

child

_____

helper(s)

_____

did this activity together

_____and

child

_____

helper(s)

_____

did this activity together

Not now, Bernard

● When do your parents tell you 'Not now...'?

● Write a comic strip based on the story **Not now, Bernard** with you in the story instead of Bernard. Use pictures and words.

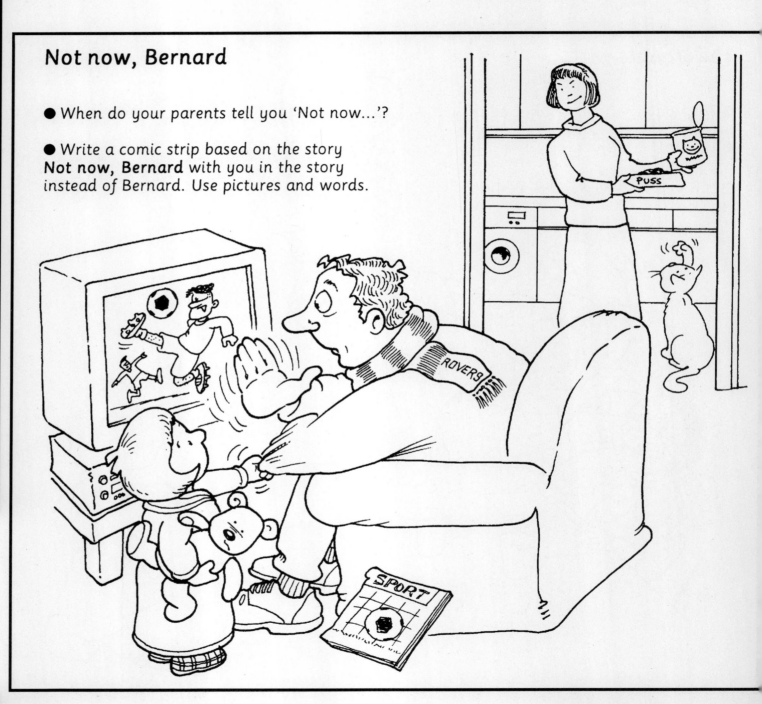

Leaving home

● Imagine that you are fed up with everyone, and you have decided to leave home. Write a list of all the things you would pack in your bag.

Make sure that you can fit all these things in one bag!

To the helper:

● Many children at some point or other decide they want to leave home. Talk about the things they would need to pack, for example money, wash things, warm clothes etc. You may want to talk about the impracticalities, and even the dangers of leaving home.
● If the list gets very long, take over with the writing. Don't worry about the spellings on this activity, getting the ideas down on paper is more important.

Writing lists is a very important skill for children to learn for sorting and organising information.

_____and

child

_____

helper(s)

_____

did this activity together

_____and

child

_____

helper(s)

_____

did this activity together

School likes and dislikes

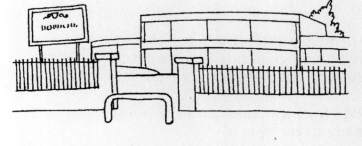

● What do you like about school?

● What don't you like about school?

● Write down a list of things you do and do not like about school.

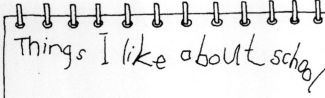

Things I like about school

Things I don't like about school

Call 999!

● Draw a picture of a time when you might need to dial 999.
(You can make something up.)

● Write down what you would have to say to the operator.

To the helper:

- Talk about all of the emergency services; can your child name all of them?
- You might need to remind your child what questions they will be asked on the other end of the phone, so they can think what they would reply. For example, do they know their own address?

It is always useful to think what you might do in an emergency before it happens! This activity gives the children a chance to think through their own actions, before writing them down.

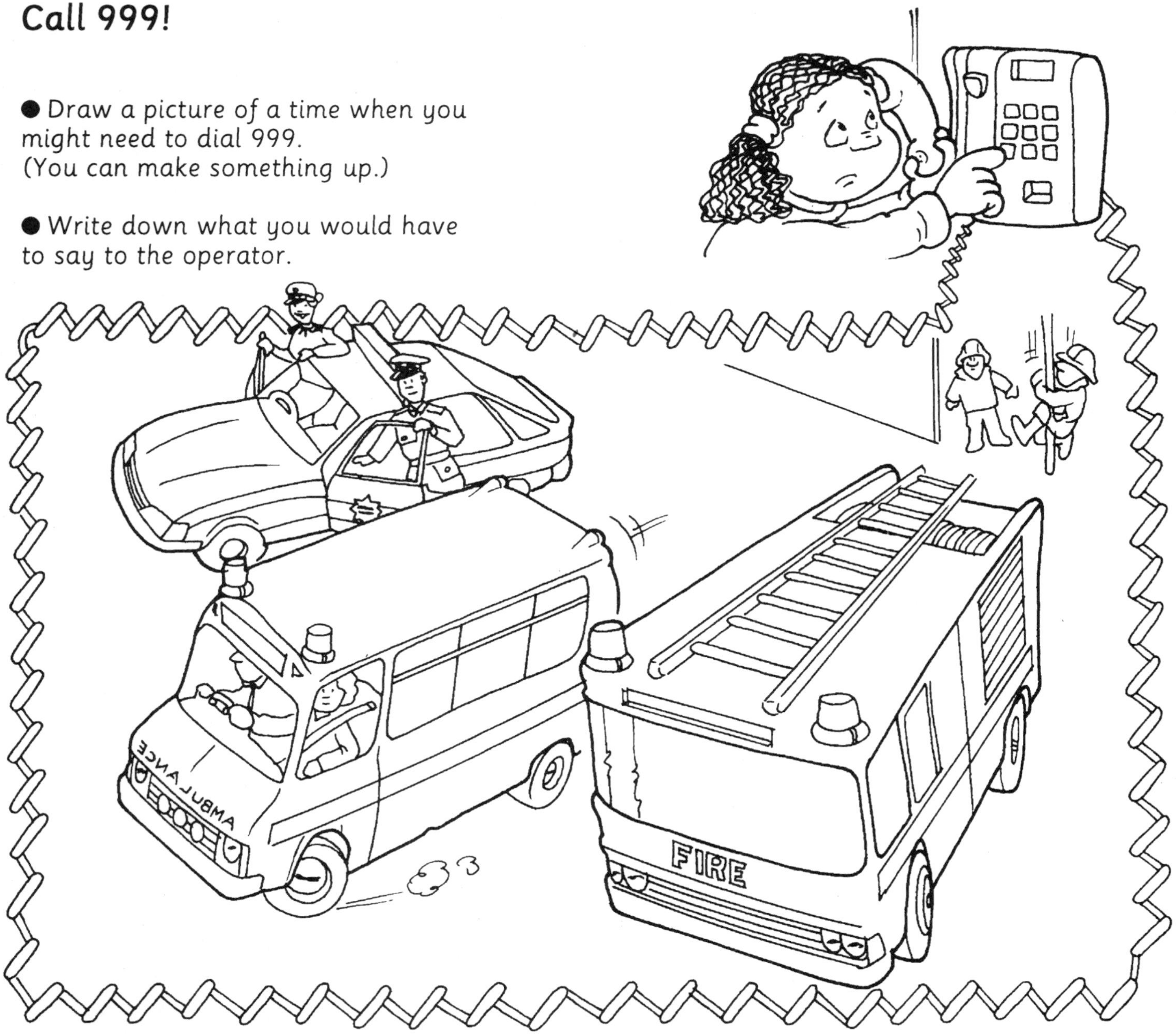

______________________ and
child

____
helper(s)

____

did this activity together

To the helper:

● Talk about your child's accident, you probably will not have to help them remember!
● Give a hand with the writing if necessary.
● You could tell them about any nasty accidents you had as a child; have either of you ever had to go to hospital after an accident?

Recalling an experience like this brings back many feelings and emotions. When the children write their own stories, and develop characters, they will need to be able to draw on their own experiences to create believable characters, or plots.

_____and

child

_____

helper(s)

_____

did this activity together

The day I fell over!

● Have you ever had a bad fall or accident?

● Draw a picture of the worst fall or accident you have ever had.

● Write a sentence about it underneath.

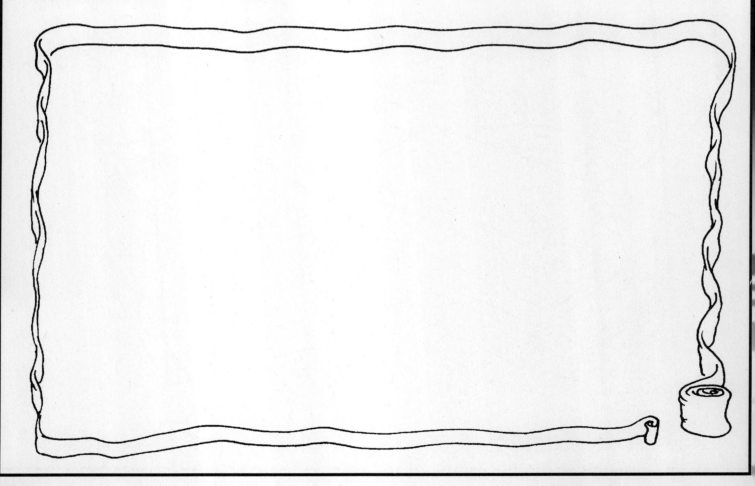

Advice to an old woman

The old woman who lived in a shoe had so many children she didn't know what to do. Ask your Mum or Dad for some advice for the old woman; what could she do with all those children?

● Write down two ideas.

To the helper:

● Go over the nursery rhyme so that you are both familiar with it.

● Talk about the things you like to do in the holidays; perhaps you could think of some fun things to do, and some *useful* things to do, like tidying up or cleaning!

We shall collect all of these ideas together in the class to make a class book of *holiday ideas*.

_____ and

child

_____

helper(s)

_____

did this activity together

_____and

child

_____

helper(s)

_____

did this activity together

When I grow up...

● Imagine something you would like to be or do when you are grown up.

● Ask your helper to help you write about it.

● Draw a picture.

Teddy bear's picnic

Imagine the Teddy Bear's picnic basket...

- Draw two things that you think might be in it.
- Write down what they are.

_____and

child

_____

helper(s)

_____

did this activity together

_____and

child

_____

helper(s)

_____

did this activity together

Puppet presenter

● Imagine children's BBC need an idea for a new puppet presenter. Can you think of one?

● What do you think the puppet should do?

● Draw a picture of your new presenter, and write down its name.

Shopping lists

● Who is your favourite character from a book?

● Imagine that you have to collect your character's shopping. What kind of things will be on the shopping list?

To the helper:

● First of all, choose a character, and then talk about the sort of things the person might need on a weekly visit to the shops. Think about the food they might like to eat, and other things like pet food, or things for the house they might need.

Writing lists is a very important skill for children to learn for sorting and organising information. We shall collect all the shopping lists together at school, and see if we can guess one another's characters from the lists.

_____and

child

_____

helper(s)

_____

did this activity together

_____and

child

_____

helper(s)

_____

did this activity together

Door plate

● Design a sign to go on your bedroom door.

● What do you want it to say?

● Will it have a picture as well?

For example, Scientist at work!
                    No noise before 8am!

Badges!

- Design a badge or sticker.

- What will it say?

- Will it be funny or serious?
How many words do you use?

- Draw a good picture to go on it.

To the helper:

- Do you have any badges or stickers at home? Look at these to help you with ideas.
- Think about the stickers and badges that you see people wearing – sometimes they have a particular message.
  - to promote a charity;
  - to tell a joke;

By designing a badge children are having to write a message or joke in a short, concise and eye-catching way – badges are supposed to attract people's attention, and get them talking. We shall talk about and display the badges when they get back to school.

_____and

child

_____

helper(s)

_____

did this activity together

_____and

child

_____

helper(s)

_____

did this activity together

T-shirt

● Make a design to go on a T-shirt.

● Use at least three words and a picture.

● Make it one that everyone will want to wear.

● Draw a picture of it.

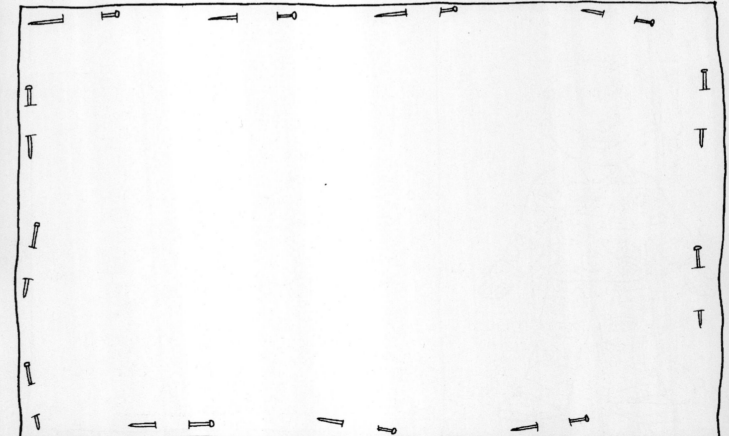

impact WRITING HOMEWOR

Horses for courses

- If you had a pet elephant, what name would you give it?

- If you had a pet snake, what name would you give that?

- Think of a peculiar pet. Draw it, and give it a suitable name.
Write down the name.

_____and

child

_____

helper(s)

_____

did this activity together

_____and

child

_____

helper(s)

_____

did this activity together

What a shock!

● Has something ever made you jump? Or given you a fright?

● Draw a picture and write down what it was.

impact WRITING HOMEWOR

Rainbow's end

● Imagine that you have reached the bottom of the rainbow. Instead of a pot of gold, you find another treasure. What is it?

● Draw a picture and write down what it is that you find.

_____and

child

_____

helper(s)

_____

did this activity together

_____and

child

_____

helper(s)

_____

did this activity together

A new ride at the fair

● Here is a roundabout with a difference.

● Give it a name so that people will want to go on it.

● Draw a picture of your favourite ride at the fair.

impact WRITING HOMEWOR

Animal crackers!

- Have you ever known an animal to do a funny thing?

- Ask your helper to write about it with you, and draw a picture.

_____and

child

_____

helper(s)

_____

did this activity together

_____and

child

_____

helper(s)

did this activity together

Horrid cake

● What things would you put in a **horrid cake**?

● Write a list of the ingredients.

(It must be edible, and not poisonous, but it can taste really horrible!)

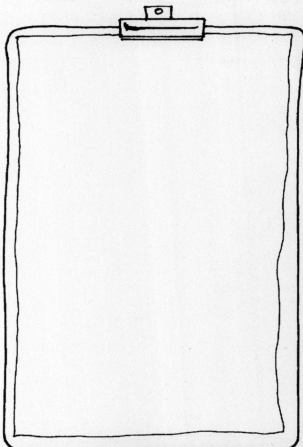

Animal nanny

In Peter Pan the children are looked after by a big furry dog.

● If you had to have an **animal nanny**, which animal would you choose to have?

● Draw a picture and write a sentence about your nanny, saying why your animal would be a good choice as a nanny.

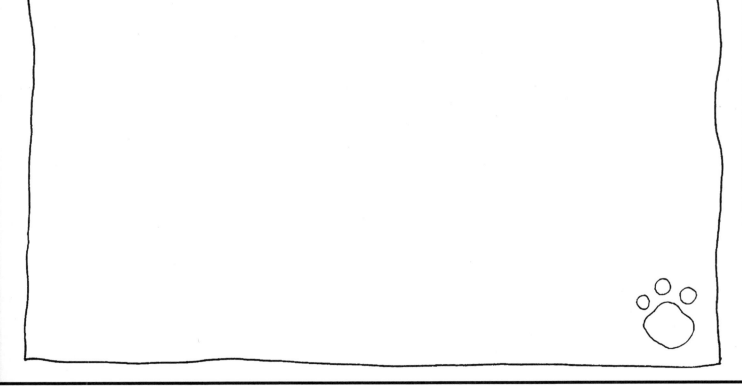

_____and

child

_____

helper(s)

_____

did this activity together

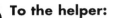

Teachers' Notes
YEAR TWO

Headline stories Collect lots of different newspaper headlines. Ask the children to work in groups and sort their headlines according to the number of words. Can they find a real newspaper headline that has the same number of words as theirs? Do any headlines have several words that start with the same letter? Now look at the headlines and try to make a link between the headlines and the stories. Hold up the headlines so the children can see how they are written, and read them for themselves. Can they guess what the story is? Finally, display the work alongside real newspapers.

Noah's notices These notices can make a wonderful display around a big picture of the ark. Read out some of the notices to the children. Can they guess which animals the notices are for? Has anyone thought of any unusual animals? A good book to read to the children before or after this activity is *Trouble in the Ark* by Gerald Rose (Bodley Head) which tells an alternative Noah story. The trouble is caused by the animals misbehaving. Back in class, the children could imagine what might happen if their particular rule was not followed on the ark. These stories could then be collected into a class book.

Storybook hotseat Talk about what a main character is, and discuss the ones that have been chosen by the children. Sort the characters; are they good or bad, brave or a coward, ugly or beautiful, etc? You may

find that most of the characters are 'good'; why are most main characters good? When you next read a story to the class, take some time to 'hotseat' one of the characters from your story. The first time you do this you take the role of the character, and get the children to ask you their questions, answering for the character. Once the children have the idea, they can take turns to answer questions in the role of a character themselves.

Down my street At home, this activity will have provoked a lot of discussion about a range of characters. When the children bring back their character names, share either in groups, or with the whole class, their reasons for their choices. This could then be followed up by drawing pictures of what they think the character's house might look like if they could build one to suit the character. This activity will fit in with any work on the local environment, houses or homes.

Storybook storyboard Read the storyboards together; perhaps you could pair the children up to hear one another's stories. The work can then be displayed in a class book. You could follow up the activity by giving a different story to each group of four or five children in the class, and getting them to retell the story with a picture each in the style of a storyboard. If the pictures are large enough these can then be displayed along the wall for the other children to read. This can be a useful way in for children to make their own storybooks – dividing up the story into pages is sometimes the most difficult part!

Breakfast noises Collect all the sounds the children have written down. You might want to point out any example of onomatopoeia that the children have used or invented, but also you can now use this collection to draw on for breakfast-noises poems. An hilarious but graphic version of this is *Shut your mouth when you're eating!*

by Michael Rosen in *Quick let's get out of here!* (Penguin) – it gives a wonderful example of the kinds of conversations that happen at mealtimes.

Invisible colour In class the children can swap their descriptions. Can they guess what the objects being described are? They must not be told the colours.

No hesitations! When the children bring their descriptions back into the classroom, they can swap descriptions. Can they guess what the objects being described are? Can the children write some of their descriptions and draw a picture of the object. The pictures and descriptions can be mounted and placed in a display. Can other people guess which drawing goes with which description?

Rules 1–4 When the children bring their 'Golden Rules' back into the classroom, talk about a few of them altogether. Next group the children to discuss one another's rules, and how they might have changed the story. Does anyone have a rule that stops the story altogether? Get each group to choose three or four of the best rules, and then to re-tell the story. Each group could then record their story in the form of a short play. This work could link very well with work on rules and safety such as the *Green Cross Code*.

Wanted poster 1 Follow up this work by writing a newspaper report on the capture and punishment of the wolf. It might be fun to consider what kind of punishment the three little pigs would choose to inflict on the wolf, given the opportunity!

Wanted poster 2 Follow up with work on a newspaper report on the arrest and punishment of the step-sisters. It might be fun to consider what kind of punishment Cinderella would choose to inflict on them, given the opportunity! Babette Cole's *Prince Cinders* (Picture Lions Armada) tells another version of the same story where the big and hairy step-brothers get their just desserts!

Wanted poster 3 Follow up by writing a newspaper report on the capture and punishment of Goldilocks. Consider what kind of punishment the three bears would choose to inflict on Goldilocks, given the opportunity!

Announcements 1–2 A nice way to follow up the work that the children will have done at home writing their announcements would be to read *The Jolly Postman* by Janet and Allan Ahlberg (Heinemann) which uses very similar ways to tell the story of a postman as he delivers letters to all the characters in fairytale land.

Story starts Talk with the children about which story starts they thought were the most intriguing; would they choose one they had written, or the original one in the book? The next time you are story writing with the children, split the class into groups, each one to use a different story start at the beginning of their story. Change the groups each time you write stories, so they get a chance to use each of the styles. Alternatively, you could incorporate them into any whole-class story writing you do, choosing a different style each time.

Rumplestiltskin Make some pictures of these weird and wonderful characters – display them next to their names. Next talk about the children's characters. What are they like? Where do they live? What do they do? Put the children in pairs and get them to invent stories around their characters – try to get both characters in each story. Perhaps these could be written as joint zigzag books that they could then read to the rest of the class.

Silly stories Talk about how the children changed their pages. What other nonsense sentences can they write? Start them off with examples like 'I came in very tired and I sat down on my favourite banana!' or 'It was a nice day so Mr Gumpy took his ice-cream out for a walk on its lead.'

et each child write one nonsense sentence and illustrate it with a funny picture. These can make a lovely display.

Speech bubbles Talk about the ways different characters talk. How do the children imagine an old man talking? What about a young man? How do they think animals might talk, if they could. Let each child draw a picture of their favourite animal and write something in a speech bubble next to it. These pictures can make a nice display or class book.

What happened was... Follow this work up through the use of role-play. You can be the first candidate; choose one of the children's stories, or use one of your own, and tell the story as if telling a friend. Write down your first sentence. Then ask one of the children if they can tell their story. Write down their opening sentence. Collect a few; hopefully they will be different. These can now be stored as a resource in the classroom for unusual story starts. Another idea could be to get the children to tell one another their stories in pairs. Emphasise that they need to concentrate on what the other person is saying, because in a minute they are going to have to pretend to be that person, and retell their story just as they said it!

Whoopsadaisy! Read the storyboards together; perhaps you could pair the children up to hear one another's stories. The work can then be displayed in a class book. You could follow up the activity by giving a different story to each group or four or five children in the class, and getting them to retell the story with a picture each in the style of a storyboard. If the pictures are large enough these can then be displayed along the wall for the other children to read. This can be a useful way in for children to make their own storybooks – dividing up the story into pages is sometimes the most difficult part!

Born again! Read out the children's announcements anonymously, and see if the children can identify one another from their own descriptions. You could ask the children to bring in photos of themselves as babies, and display these with the appropriate announcements.

Pratt-s! Talk about the names that the children have chosen; how have they made their names sound suitably scary or weird? Try writing some scary stories in the classroom, and get the children to imagine which part they might play in their story. A further extension of this might be to design the costume, or the set for a particularly scary part of their story.

I don't like it! Use the lists of disgusting words as a resource for the times when you run out of adjectives (or you keep seeing the same ones!). These can also be used for making horrible food pictures, a menu for a monster etc.

I was late for school because... A wonderful book to read either before or after you send this task home is *John Henry....* The tall stories that the children have written at home could be mounted in a class book that has been made suitably long and thin; a tall book for tall stories! Can the children think of reasons why the *teachers* might be late for school?

Come away from the water, Shirley! Read the book together first in school. This activity will fit in well with any work to do with either letter-writing or holidays. To display both sides at once place the postcards into a clear plastic file. The children can then flick through the file and look at both sides of the cards.
Come away from the water, Shirley! John Burningham (Red Fox)

It's a bear! Share all the scary stories together (or a selection). Use the children's ideas in short plays about creeping up on and discovering a scary animal, and what happens next! It might be fun to pool all the

best ideas into a class version of *We're going on a bear hunt!*, complete with actions that you could use in an assembly or short presentation to another class.

What I like Talk in class about rhyming couplets beforehand. Their ideas could easily be incorporated into a class poem of what they like. Write this out in large, clear writing and display it for the children to read (they will find it hard to resist going up to it to find their own two lines!) This is only one form of the many different ways of writing poetry, so make sure that the activity is not done in isolation; read a wide selection of different styles to the children, and talk about them.

Where the Wild Things Are Discuss what punishments children think are fair. Which do they think are most unfair? Suppose they were in charge of someone younger than them. What punishments do they think they would want to give if the child was naughty? Ask them to write a few sentences about which punishment they would use.

Household tasks This might be a good opportunity to talk about parents or carers, and the work they do at home which is sometimes invisible to the children they care for. If you have sent this activity home in the run up to Christmas, Easter or another festival, it would be nice to incorporate a thank you into the card or present they are taking home; or if not, the children could write thank you letters home.

Favourite clothes This activity will tie in with work about clothes, or family history. Display the pictures of the children in their favourite outfits, and talk about the kinds of things their parents used to wear when they were their age. How are they different? What kinds of things did they wear? What items of clothing don't you see any more? What items of clothing weren't even invented when their parents were children? (Eg bum bags, specialised trainers etc.)

What things might not have been around when their grandparents were children?

That's not fair! Ask the children to justify why they thought their rules were sensible. Talk about why they think it is necessary to have rules at all. Did anyone write down any rules that they think are unfair? Are there any rules at your school that the children think are unfair, and why? You could use this opportunity to write some classroom rules, or a class charter listing a few statements to which all members of the class agree to adhere.

Midnight owls You may want to assemble the stories as they are into a 'midnight adventures book', or you could use these as a first draft for a more carefully presented and expanded version of their stories. Use the first few that come back as a starting point for discussing the way they could polish up, or elaborate on their stories. Collect phrases and adjectives that are particularly evocative of the midnight hour. Don't forget the large selection of children's literature written on this theme, for example *Midnight Teddies* by Dana Kubrick (Walker Books), *Tom's Midnight Garden* by Philippa Pearce (Penguin), etc.

Table manners This activity should initiate some interesting discussions at home, and give parents an opportunity to have a moan about all the annoying things their children do while sitting at the dinner table! Talk about the kinds of things they have written down, and collect them all together. Michael Rosen, in his book *Don't put mustard in the custard!* (Picture Lions) has written a poem of the same title which illustrates the kinds of things children might hear their parents saying to them (tongue in cheek). It provides a useful frame into which the children can fit their own 'moans' from their parents.

_____and

child

_____

helper(s)

did this activity together

Headline stories

● Rewrite the title of your reading book in the style of a newspaper headline.

For example: Blonde girl wrecks Bear Family Home. 'We demand an apology' stated Mr Bear.

● Which story does this come from?

Noah's notices

There were probably hundreds of animals on Noah's Ark. It must have been very difficult keeping everything in order!

Imagine that the animals could read.

● Design a notice that Noah might have put up on the ark wall for them.

To the helper:

● Ask your child about the story of Noah, and talk about all the animals that might have been on board.

● Let your child have a go at the writing, but do take over if necessary.

This activity will help the children develop their own imaginative story writing. Through adding details to a traditional story, the children are made to concentrate on an imagined picture of the ark in their mind, and fill in details that are not included in the original story.

_____and

child

_____

helper(s)

_____

did this activity together

_____and

child

_____

helper(s)

_____

did this activity together

Storybook hotseat

● Who are the main characters in the storybook you are reading tonight?

Pretend that you are going to meet these characters.

● Write down a list of the questions you would ask them.

Think of things that you would like to know about them, or why they did certain things in the story.

Down my street

● Ask your helper to help you write down the name of a fairy story character who you would like to have living down your street!

_____and

child

_____

helper(s)

_____

did this activity together

_____and

child

_____

helper(s)

did this activity together

Storybook storyboard

● Read your story book carefully tonight, and then think how you might show the story in the form of a storyboard.

● Re-tell your story in a five or six frame storyboard.

Breakfast noises

LISTEN!

● What noises can you hear when you eat your breakfast?

● Think of some good words to describe the sounds.

● Write down a list of the noises.

To the helper:

● You could talk about the sounds inside and outside the house, for example; a telephone ringing, a baby crying etc. You could also concentrate on the sounds they can hear while they are actually eating their breakfast!

Making children concentrate on just one of their senses helps them to focus on their immediate surroundings, and what is happening around them. Putting words to these sounds makes the picture even clearer, especially when describing the situation to someone else. Back in class we will use these ideas to write poems.

_____and

child

_____

helper(s)

_____

did this activity together

_____and

child

_____

helper(s)

_____

did this activity together

Invisible colour

Play this with your helper.

● Choose a colour, for example green.

● Now take it in turns to give the other person an object of that colour to describe. They must describe that object without saying the chosen colour. For example, I must describe a cucumber without using the word 'green'.

● Write down each description!

● Have three turns each and bring your descriptions into school.

No hesitations!

● Take it in turns to play this game.

● Each person must write a description of an object given them by the other person in no more than ten words!

For example, I tell you to describe 'a cat'!

● You write: 'Walking furry four-legged animal, whiskers and miaows. Eats fish.'

To the helper:

● This is more difficult than it looks! Try playing the game a few times without the limitations of ten words or less, just to get the hang of it.
● Help with the writing if necessary.

This game makes the children use describing words and phrases that they might not usually choose to use in their normal spoken or written work. The children will have to exercise describing skills that are generally under-used!

_____and

child

_____

helper(s)

_____

did this activity together

impact WRITING HOMEWORK

_____and

child

_____

helper(s)

_____

did this activity together

Rules 1

● Think of some sensible rules to help the three little pigs, so that they could escape the Big Bad Wolf!

● Write down five **Golden rules** for them, and tell someone how the story might have been different if they had kept these rules!

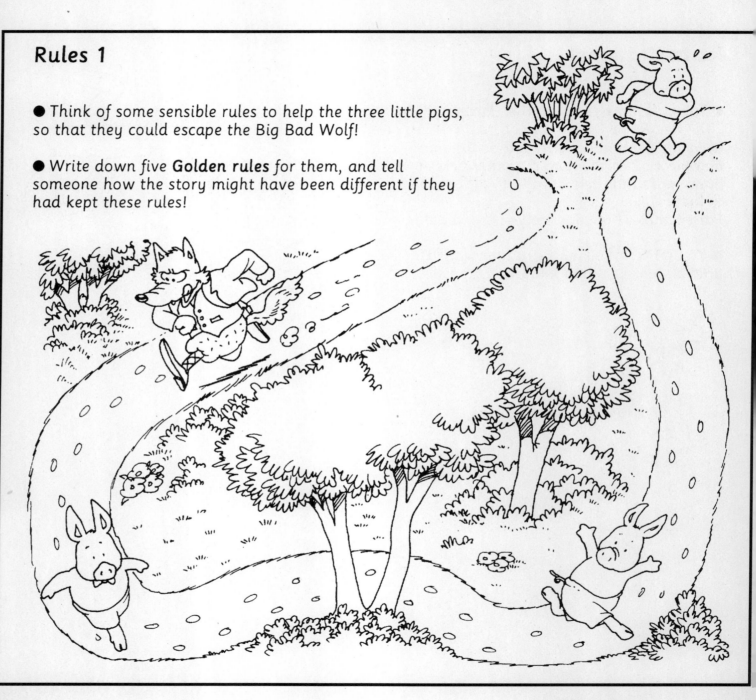

Rules 2

● Think of some sensible rules that might have helped Little Red Riding Hood escape from the Big Bad Wolf!

● Write down five **Golden rules** for her, and tell someone how the story might have been different if she had kept to these rules!

To the helper:

● You will need to talk about the story together; remembering all the things that Little Red Riding Hood did – perhaps your child can think what they would have done if a stranger came up to them.

● If you talk for a long time, and if the rules are quite long, you may find that you need to take over with the writing.

By doing this, it will help your child realise that stories are not fixed and permanent, but *made up* and changed by people's telling of them. Also, rule-writing in itself requires a specific sense of style, and an understanding of whom the rules are for.

_____and

child

_____

helper(s)

_____

did this activity together

_____and

child

_____

helper(s)

_____

did this activity together

Rules 3

● Think of some sensible house rules that might have helped Goldilocks, so that she would not have been so naughty in the house of the three bears.

● Write down three **Golden rules** for her, and tell someone how the story might have been different if she had kept to these rules!

Rules 4

● Think of some sensible rules that might have helped the Billy Goats Gruff, so that they could have escaped the troll!

● Write down five **Golden rules** for them, and tell someone how the story might have been different if they had kept to these rules!

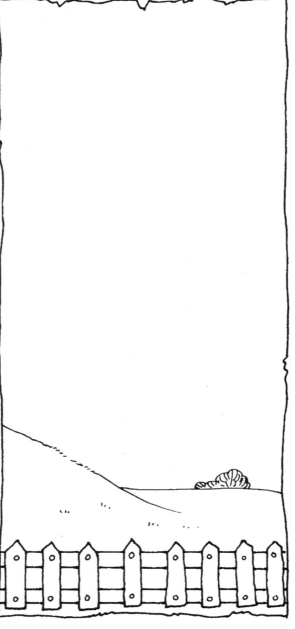

_____and

child

_____

helper(s)

_____

did this activity together

_____and

child

_____

helper(s)

_____

did this activity together

Wanted poster 1

Imagine that you work for the police in fairy tale land.

You are in charge of issuing descriptions, and designing **wanted** posters for all criminals.

● Design a poster that includes a good description of the Big Bad Wolf and a brief description of his crime.

(You might even think of a good reward for any information leading to an arrest!)

Wanted poster 2

Imagine that you work for the police in fairy tale land.

You are in charge of issuing descriptions, and designing **wanted** posters for all criminals.

● Design a poster that includes a good description of Cinderella's step-sisters, with a brief description of their crimes.

To the helper:

● Help with the writing if necessary.
● Talk about the style of a wanted poster, for example, the type often used in westerns.

This activity will encourage the children to think carefully about the characters of the two sisters and also about the style and presentation of a wanted poster.

_____and

child

_____

helper(s)

_____

did this activity together

impact WRITING HOMEWORK

_____and

child

_____

helper(s)

_____

did this activity together

Wanted poster 3

Imagine that you work for the police in fairy tale land.

You are in charge of issuing descriptions and designing **wanted** posters for all criminals.

● Design a poster that includes a good description of Goldilocks and a brief description of her crime(s).

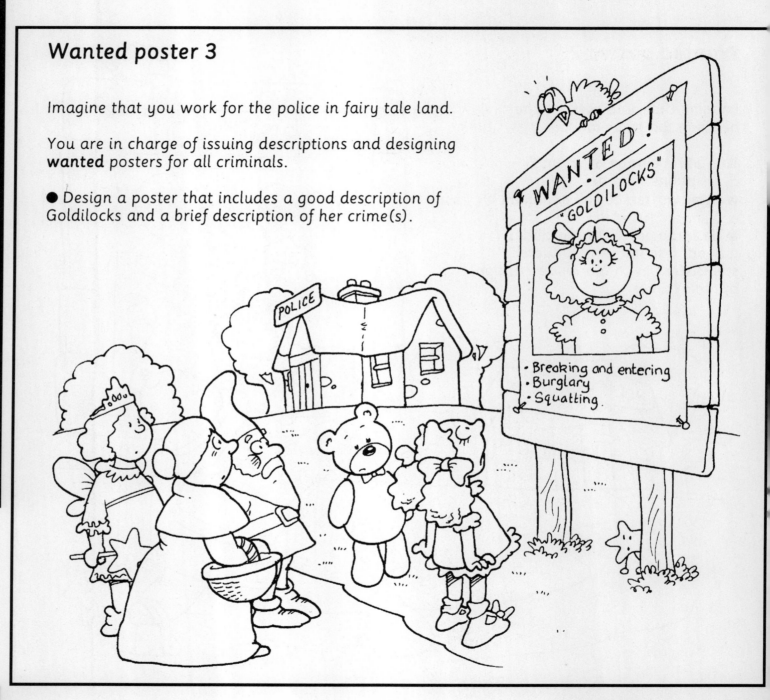

Announcements 1

Look at a newspaper with your helper, and see if you can find the **Announcements** column.

Let your helper read you a few of the announcements.

● Together, try to write an announcement for a newspaper to let everyone know that Prince Charming and Cinderella are to be married.

To the helper:

● Talk about the style of writing used in announcement columns; compare it with, for example, a story or the writing in a birthday card.

● Say your announcement out loud first, and then try to write it down; if this part becomes too drawn-out, and your child becomes tired or loses interest, take over with the writing.

Writing for different purposes demands different styles of writing. This activity will draw your child's attention to a specific style of writing, through the story of Cinderella.

_____and

child

_____

helper(s)

_____

did this activity together

To the helper:

- Talk about the style of writing used in announcement columns; compare it with, for example, a story or the writing in a birthday card.
- Say your announcement out loud first, and then try to write it down; if this part becomes too drawn-out, and your child becomes tired or loses interest, take over with writing.

Writing for different purposes demands different styles of writing. This activity will draw your child's attention to a specific style of writing, through the story of Little Red Riding Hood.

_____and

child

_____

helper(s)

_____

did this activity together

Announcements 2

Look at a newspaper with your helper, and see if you can find the **Announcements** column.

Let your helper read you a few of the announcements.

● Together, try to write an announcement for a newspaper to let everyone know that the Big Bad Wolf has been killed by the woodcutter.

Story starts

● How does the story in your reading book start?

Does it have:
• a traditional beginning, for example
'Once upon a time...' or 'There was once a...'
• a general statement, for example
'Teachers can be so annoying...'
• setting the scene, for example
'When I was just sitting down...'
• a dramatic start, for example
'Bang! The door slammed behind me...'

● Which type of beginning does it have or does it have another sort?

● Try re-writing the first sentence in your reading book in each of the four styles described above.

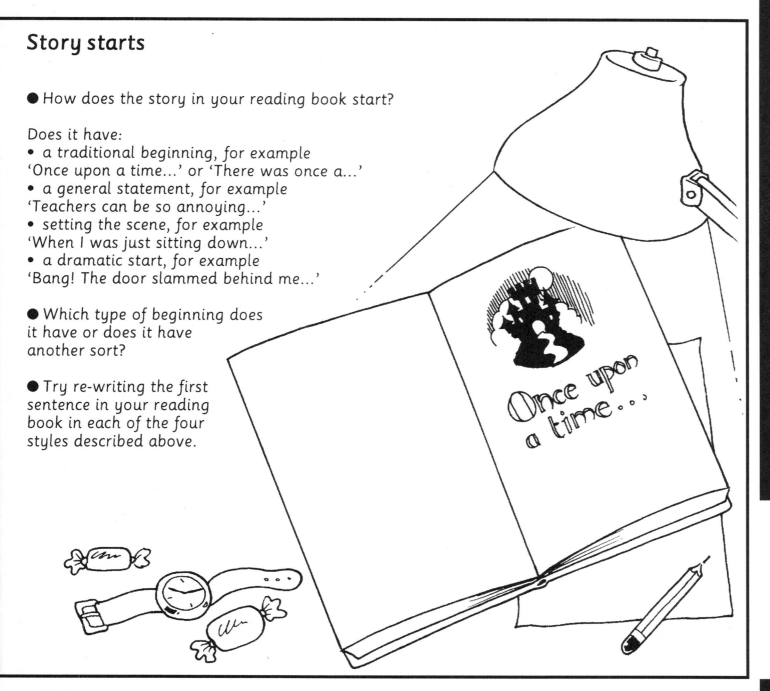

To the helper:

● It may not be immediately obvious which type of *Story start* the story book has, so spend a little time talking together about the different categories before you decide.
● Help with the spelling if necessary.

By re-writing the start of their story, the children are trying different styles, which they might not have used before. This will provide them with a broader repertoire of story starts to choose from for when they write their own stories.

_____and

child

_____

helper(s)

_____

did this activity together

_____and

child

_____

helper(s)

_____

did this activity together

Rumplestiltskin

● Isn't Rumplestiltskin a fantastic name! Would you have ever guessed it?

● Make up some other fantastic names that might appear in story books. Try to think of four or five. (Your helper could help you write them down.)

Silly stories

● Go through part of a story (for example from your reading book), and change a few words with your helper, so that the story becomes a nonsense one!

For example:
We changed a few words from a page in **Dogger** by Shirley Hughes (Red Fox).

Once there was a **spikey green** toy called Dogger. One of his **toes** pointed upwards and the other flopped over. His fur was worn in places because he was quite **noisy**. He belonged to **Superman**.

● Can you see which words have been changed?

● See if you can do the same kind of thing with a page from your book. (Get your helper to write down the words you don't want to change.)

To the helper:

● Talk about which page would be a good one to work on. It is probably best to choose one without too many words!

Thinking about what _makes sense_ and what is _nonsense_ is important. Humour often relies on this distinction and the children can be very inventive and creative in thinking up _nonsense_ sentences which are none-the-less grammatical.

_____and

child

_____

helper(s)

_____

did this activity together

_____and

child

_____

helper(s)

_____

did this activity together

Speech bubbles

● Draw a character from your picture book.

● Cut out the speech bubble, or the thought bubble, and put it next to a character in your picture book.

● Write in the bubble what you think the person is thinking or saying here.

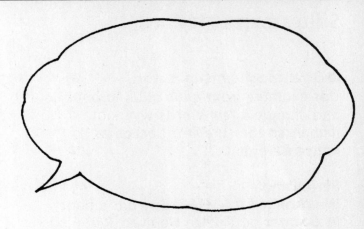

What happened was...

● Talk about an incident or event which has happened in your life that was important or unusual.

For example, something good like a special visit on holiday or something bad like an accident.

● Write about it like this:
• you write one sentence;
• your helper writes a sentence;
• you write a sentence;
• your helper writes a sentence...

To the helper:

● Talk about important events; you might need to help your child remember!
● Help with the writing if necessary.
● You could tell your child about any special events you remember as a child.

Remembering an experience like this brings back valuable feelings and emotions. When the children are writing their own stories, and developing characters, they will need to be able to draw on their own experiences to create believable characters or plots.

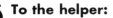

_____and

child

_____

helper(s)

_____

did this activity together

_____and

child

_____

helper(s)

_____

did this activity together

Whoopsadaisy!

● Are you ever clumsy?

● Do you know anyone who is often clumsy?

● Think of a time when you, or someone you know, was clumsy.

● Talk about it with your helper and design a cartoon strip to tell the story.

Born again!

● How did your parents tell everyone that you were born?

● Some people put an announcement in the newspaper. If you were being born now, how would you like it to be announced in the newspaper?

_____and

child

_____

helper(s)

_____

did this activity together

_____and

child

_____

helper(s)

_____

did this activity together

Pratt – s!

Boris Karloff was a famous horror movie star, but his real name was William Pratt.

● If you were a horror movie star what name would you choose for yourself?

● Draw a picture of yourself in the horror movie, and write your **stage name** underneath.

I don't like it!

● What foods do you hate?

● Talk to the others in your house; what foods do they hate?

● Write a list of some of them.

● Think of three words to describe the food you most dislike.

To the helper:

● Talk about these foods, and help with writing the list.

● Talk about the thing you both hate the most (this might be two things), and brainstorm as many *disgusting* words as you can think of, and choose the three best ones.

Writing lists is a very important skill for children to learn for sorting and organising information. Brainstorming adjectives will help them think about alternatives to the rather over-used few that tend to be chosen over and over again when children write.

_____and

child

_____

helper(s)

_____

did this activity together

_____and

child

_____

helper(s)

_____

did this activity together

I was late for school because...

● Can you and your helper both think of two excuses why you might have been late for school?

● Make the tales as **tall** as possible.

● Write down one of your stories and illustrate it.

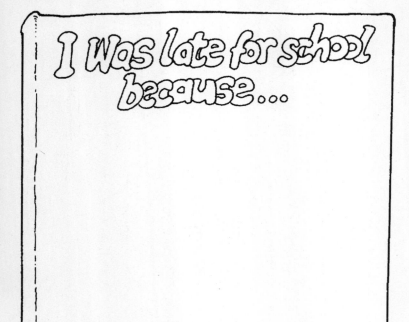

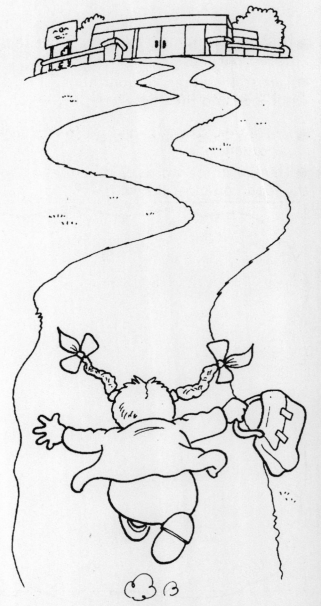

Come away from the Water, Shirley!

- Tell the story of **Come away from the Water, Shirley** to your helper.

- Imagine you are Shirley on holiday.

- Write a postcard home to a friend, telling them about your **adventures**.

_____and

child

_____

helper(s)

_____

did this activity together

_____and

child

_____

helper(s)

_____

did this activity together

It's a bear!

Michael Rosen writes:

One shiny wet nose,
   Two big goggly eyes...
      ...It's a bear!

● Could you write something similar to this about another animal or monster that might scare you?

● Imagine that you creep up on them like **We're going on a Bear Hunt**, and then discover what they are.

● Write down your ideas, and draw a picture.

What I like

● With your helper write a poem in rhyming couplets about things you like. Each line must rhyme, for example:

'Lying on a beach on a hot summer's day
Playing X-Men figures when my brother's gone away'

● These two lines end with an **-ay** sound, the next two lines could rhyme with a different sound. Ask your helper to help you write the poem down.

To the helper:

● Help with the writing, and if needed, with ideas for rhyming words.

This activity gives the children experience of a particular kind of poetry writing, which in turn makes them use their knowledge about rhyming words.

_____and

child

_____

helper(s)

_____

did this activity together

_____and

child

_____

helper(s)

_____

did this activity together

Where the Wild Things Are

Max was sent to his room without his supper. He went to the land where the Wild Things are.

● What is your most hated punishment?

● Write it down.

● Tell the story of **Where the Wild Things Are** to your helper, and ask them what their most hated punishment was when they were a child.

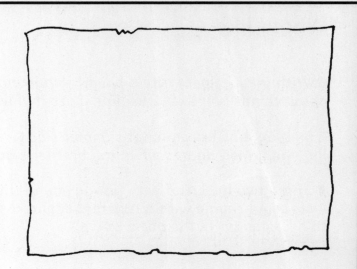

Household tasks

● What do you do to help around the house?

● Write a list of the jobs you sometimes help with.

● Find out which jobs your helper hates doing the most!

_____and

child

_____

helper(s)

_____

did this activity together

_____and

child

_____

helper(s)

_____

did this activity together

Favourite clothes

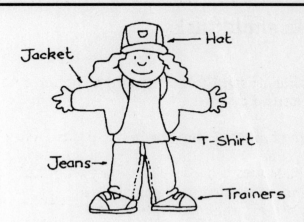

Jacket · Hat · T-Shirt · Jeans · Trainers

● What do you most like to wear?

● Draw a picture of yourself in your favourite outfit, and label all the clothes.

● Ask your helper: what was your favourite outfit when you were my age?

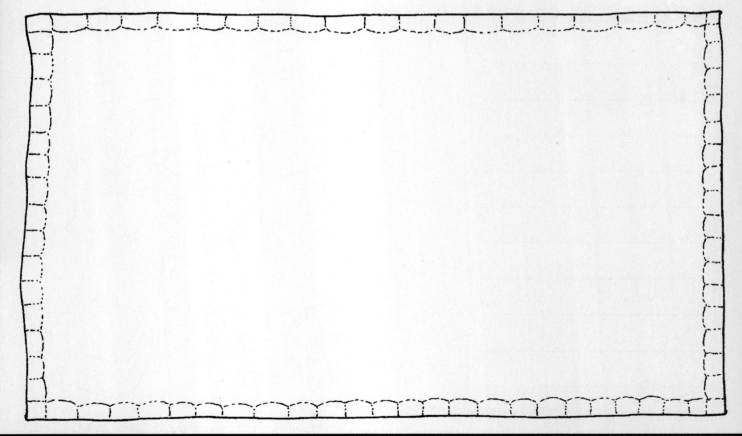

That's not fair!

- Make a list of three things that you are not allowed to do.

- Which ones do you think are unfair? Why?

- Which ones do you think are fair? Why?

To the helper:

- Talk about why rules are important; what might happen if you had no rules in your house?

We shall use these back in class when writing possible imaginary scenarios, exploring the necessary rules for living together. Making lists is an excellent organisational skill which helps children plan their writing.

_____and

child

_____

helper(s)

_____

did this activity together

_____and

child

_____

helper(s)

_____

did this activity together

Midnight owls

● Have you ever been awake at midnight?

● Write about a time when you stayed up really late.

impact WRITING HOMEWORK

Table manners

- Can you hang a spoon on the end of your nose?

- Can you balance peas on the back of your fork?

- What do you like doing at the table that annoys your parents?

- Write down some of the things you do.

To the helper:

- Tell your child all the things they do which really annoy you at the dinner table; but try to keep it light-hearted! Do you know anyone who can do anything really outrageous?

Annoying or funny things that happen at home can provide wonderful stimulation for funny poem writing. We shall use these ideas for poem writing at school.

_____and

child

_____

helper(s)

did this activity together

Management

Most teachers send the shared writing task as a photocopied sheet included in the children's **Reading Folder** or in their IMPACT **Maths folder**. Remind the children that they may use the back of the IMPACT sheet to write on. Before the activity is sent home, it is crucial that the teacher prepares the children for the task. This may involve reading a story, going over some ideas or having a group or class discussion. Some ideas are provided here in the Teachers' Notes for each activity. The importance of this preparation cannot be overstressed.

Many of the tasks done at home lend themselves naturally to a display or enable the teacher to make a class-book. A shared writing display board in the entrance hall of the school gives parents an important sense that their work at home is appreciated and valued.

The shared writing activity sheets can be stuck into an exercise book kept specifically for this purpose. Any follow-up work that the children do in school can also be put into this book. As the books go back and forth with the activity sheets this enables parents to see how the work at home has linked to work in class.

Non-IMPACTers

We know that parental support is a key factor in children's education and children who cannot find anyone with whom to share the writing task may be losing out. Try these strategies:
• Encourage, cajole and reward the children who bring back their shared writing. If a child – and parent/carer – does the task haphazardly, praise the child whenever the task is completed, rather than criticise if it does not.
• If possible, invite a couple of parents in to share the activities with the children. This involves parents in the life of the school as well as making sure that some children don't lose out.
• Some schools set up 'writing partners' between children in two different classes pairing a child from Y6 with a child in Y1 for shared writing activities, perhaps weekly or fortnightly.

None of these strategies is perfect, but many parents will help when they can and with encouragement, will join in over the longer term.

Useful information and addresses

The IMPACT shared maths scheme is running successfully in thousands of schools in the UK and abroad. The shared writing works in the same way, and obviously complements the maths very well. Both fit in with the shared reading initiatives (PACT or CAPER) which most schools in the country also run. The OFSTED Inspection Schedules require and take account of schools working with parents as well as focusing on the quality of teaching and learning. IMPACT continues to receive positive mentions in inspectors' reports.

Further information about the IMPACT Project and IMPACT inservice training for schools or parents' groups can be obtained from: The IMPACT Project, School of Teaching Studies, University of North London, 166–220 Holloway Road, London N7 8DB.

The Shared Maths Homework books can be obtained from Scholastic Ltd, Westfield Road, Southam, Nr Leamington Spa, Warwickshire CV33 0JH.

For IMPACT Diaries contact: IMPACT Supplies, PO Box 126, Witney, Oxfordshire OX8 5YL. Tel: 01993 774408.

IMPACT: Imaginative Writing: Key Stage One/ Scottish Levels A-B

The activities in this book support the following requirements for writing in the UK national curricula for English.

National Curriculum: English
1. Range – a,b,c
2. Key Skills – a,b
3. Standard English and Language Study – a,b

Scottish 5-14 Guidelines: English Language Strand	Level
Functional writing	A/B
Personal writing	A/B
Imaginative writing	A/B
Knowledge about language	B

Northern Ireland Curriculum: English
Purposes – to express thoughts, feelings, imaginings, describe, narrate. Contexts – first-hand experiences, structured play, stories, nursery rhymes, poetry. Range – variety of forms including stories, descriptions, invitations, poems, word play.